Footloose!

Other books by Brad Bird

My Dear Boy: A family's War-time letters and Memoirs from 1915 to the Kosovo Conflict (Trafford Publishing, 2011)

No Guarantees: An Inspiring Story of Struggle and Success in Professional Sport, and with Parkinson's and Cancer (Trafford, 2007)

Me and My Canoe: The Gripping Story of Paddling the Hayes and Mississippi Rivers (Pemmican Publications of Winnipeg, 2006)

Nickel Trip: A Second World War bomber pilot from Boissevain, Manitoba shares his experiences with his youngest son (Pemmican, 2004)

Footloose!

Newlyweds go walking in
England and Germany

Brad Bird

Order this book online at www.trafford.com
or email orders@trafford.com

Most Trafford titles are also available at major online book retailers.

Printed in the United States of America.

ISBN: 978-1-4269-0502-5 (sc)

Trafford rev. 06/18/2011

 www.trafford.com

North America & International
toll-free: 1 888 232 4444 (USA & Canada)
phone: 250 383 6864 ♦ fax: 812 355 4082

A Word of Thanks

The chapters about England and Germany first appeared as articles in the Oceanside Star of Parksville, British Columbia, which employed me as a reporter. I wish to thank publisher Curt Duddy, and Postmedia Community Publishing, for allowing me to reprint them and the accompanying images.

To free spirits everywhere.

Contents

The Happy Wanderer

Written by the German Friedrich-Wilhem Moller,
shortly after the Second World War.

I love to go a-wandering along the mountain track,
And as I go I love to sing, my knapsack on my back.

Chorus: Val-deri, Val-dera. Val-deri, Val-dera ha ha ha ha ha,
Val-deri, Val-dera, my knapsack on my back.

I love to wander by the stream, that dances in the sun,
So joyously it calls to me, "Come! Join my happy song!"

I wave my hand to all I meet, and they wave back to me,
And blackbirds call so loud and sweet, from every green wood tree.

High overhead the skylarks wing, they never rest at home,
But just like me, they love to sing, as o'er the world we roam.

Oh may I go a-wandering until the day I die,
Oh may I always laugh and sing
Beneath God's clear blue sky!

Introduction

Why do people wander? Because it's fun. It makes them happy. Think of all those wonderful personal encounters you've made while walking, both at home and abroad. If time is the stuff of life, as Ben Franklin once said, then people are what make that time worthwhile. Nothing picks me up or puts me in the moment as much as a friendly and interesting encounter with another human being (though cats aren't far behind!). I suppose that's why I became a journalist.

We wander because we're wired to do so. People are born to travel, to move, to seek out new places and ideas. Think of the many historic migrations over the centuries – the nomads trekking through the Middle East and Africa, the Asiatic people crossing the Bering Strait, the pioneers pushing westward in North America. What's *unnatural* is being chained to a desk day after day, as most of us are. And what a terrible price we pay for that in terms of our physical and spiritual health. But this is not a negative book.

For me, freedom is the essence of travel. I love being footloose because I love being free. I love the buzz that comes from walking. To me it's the best high of all. For some, it can take the place of pills to ward off depression. I like not knowing where I'll sleep at night, but having confidence it will be a good place. I love the freedom that comes from travel, the freedom of choice about where and how I go, what I eat, and who I spend my time with. Canoeing is almost as good as walking, and I've also done some of that. To read about my canoeing adventures across North America, check out *Me And My Canoe*.

In this book, my wife Karen Stewart and I do a lot of walking. When Karen and I set out to see England and Germany, we did so with family-related goals. We had relatives in these countries, people we needed to meet, and roots to explore. James Curtis Bird, who came to what became Canada in 1788, was born in Middlesex in London. My father, Clayton Bird, had served in England as a pilot in the 1939-45 war and was able to spend time with my mother's people in Driffield.

I wanted to meet them, and see Bournemouth where he had stayed. In Germany, Karen had family that experienced the bombing war of which dad was a part. It was important that we meet those people, and we did.

I start this book with stories about my early years, which influenced my desire to travel.

At the Winnipeg Free Press, my first big job, I was fortunate to meet some famous Canadians, whose stories I include here. I think you'll enjoy them.

Like the song says, I'm a happy wanderer. It's how God made me, and you too. I think the happy wanderer's mission is to see creation in all its glory and tell others about it – to share the joy and goodwill. This book, I hope, does some of that.

Happy wanderings!

Chapter 1

Books and the Travel Bug

Books AND MAGAZINES were all around when I was growing up in Toronto, and they definitely affected my outlook and desire to see the world. Mom and dad both read a lot. Dad, Clayton Bird, was in the Air Force until he retired in 1964, when I was five. He taught at Staff College in Toronto and wrote a book about aircraft mechanics. Before that he had flown in the war. After retirement he became a high school English teacher, so books more or less followed him around.

Mom, Doris Bird, read magazines but also enjoyed Agatha Christie novels. She and dad were married on Sept. 13, 1941. Mom was always busy with household chores but would enjoy reading *Lady's Home Journal* and similar titles. We also subscribed to *Outdoor Life, Field and Stream, Maclean's and National Geographic*. In those days, mailmen delivered stuff to your mailbox, which hung outside your front door. It had two hooks beneath it for the folded daily newspaper. Pretty well everyone read newspapers then, where we lived, either the *Toronto Daily Star* or the *Telegram* or both. We lived at 161 Grandravine Drive in Downsview, near Keele Street and Finch Avenue, close to the air base.

I badgered my parents to teach me to read when I was three or four. I knew it was the key to a bigger world for me, and the sooner I learned the better. So they got down to the business of teaching me, using the big soft-cover books then available.

My brothers also read a lot. Bil, Bob and Bruce were all older than me, with Bill being 14 when I was born in 1959. Bil swam competitively but always had a book or two on the go. I was sometimes taken along to his swim meets, but the smell of chlorine was more than I could bear. Bill also played ball, as he pitched and hit well.

Being younger, Bob and Bruce were around the house more. Bruce walked regularly in Boyd Park, where dad would drop him off for the day. There he'd track deer and walk for miles. He and Bob read *Outdoor Life* and *Field and Stream*, as dad was into fishing and hunting, which he'd learned growing up in Boissevain, Manitoba. My favourites were the true stories of adventure. "Almost Eaten by a Bear!" the headline would scream, with an image of a growling bruin on the cover. I also enjoyed reading stories about fishing for pike and bass in places like the Bay of Quinte, where we would later live. One *Outdoor Life* feature was called "This Happened to Me!" and was told in drawings with short captions to tell a story, like a comic book. Typically it was a nail-biter of an experience, either a near drowning or a close call with a truck on a mountainside or a scrape with a bear or cougar. I'd read these things, sometimes while on my belly on the floor, or curled up in a living room chair, and think of all the adventure that lay ahead when I was bigger.

National Geographic's articles weren't nearly as interesting as those in *Outdoor Life,* because it was more of a scientific journal, but the pictures were great. No other magazine compared to *National Geographic* when it came to bringing the world into your living room. People didn't travel as much in the 1960s as they do today – most couldn't afford to – and so we relied on it to tell us about foreign places and peoples. I remember reading about Morocco, and hoping to get there one day, into the Atlas Mountains. (I eventually did.) Africa was always a fascinating topic, with photos of peoples in unusual dress (or no dress, fascinating to a young lad).

But books not only told me about the world; they also taught me how to read and think.

How to Read a Book by Mortimer J. Adler was a turning point. Adler taught that you needed to find the author's main point, and also his or her outline. You needed to understand the writer's key words. You also needed to keep a few notes, or write in the margins, and question the author's premises and thinking. It all came down to being quite an active process, which was all quite new to me. It seemed like a lot of work and it was. But doing it his way improved my reading, writing and comprehension.

Two other books of note on our shelves were *The Art of Readable Writing* and *The Art of Plain Talk* by Rudolf Flesch. Flesch urged the use of short sentences, plain words, active verbs. Nobody had ever told me these things. Mind you I was only in Grade 7 or 8 when I read him, but still. Flesch's books taught these points persuasively. I didn't agree with everything he said; I felt and still feel that long sentences, properly crafted, can be easily read and understood, and that large words have a place and a time because every word has a specific meaning and occasion when it and only it is apt. But still, I liked his message. Concrete nouns – apples rather than food, Toyotas rather than automobiles, cats rather than pets – also became part of my writing style, thanks to Flesch.

In our living room, an entire wall was filled with books and magazines. Dad was handy with a saw and hammer as well as practically everything else he turned his mind to, and we didn't lack for book shelves or books to place upon them. He'd had to buy a lot of volumes while studying English to teach school after his Air Force career, and most if not all of these he kept. This was a huge bonus for us kids. There were hundreds of books but I was hooked by only a few of the classics. Partly this was because I was young. Another reason was their style; too often they failed to grab you early. That's an error on the writer's part, not the reader's.

As a kid, I found good stories in comic books. In those days there was a series called *Classic* comics, colourful stories of popular subjects like Kit Carson and Daniel Boone, American titles since this was an American company. I loved reading them. They told great stories of travel and adventure and had wonderful drawings. I came to admire Kit Carson for his daring and courage in helping open up the American West. One time he was caught out alone with an angry bear (there we go again!). He scrambled up a small tree but it bent over with his weight. As the bear approached he drew his Bowie knife and scratched its nose, scaring it away. Another time he was shot during a fight with Indians or something and the thing that saved him was the winter's cold, which slowed the bleeding. Kit Carson always seemed to escape from the jaws of danger, and he lived such an exciting life hunting buffalo and trapping beavers.

Another comic that caught my attention, and sister Kim's, was the *Archie* series. She and I made up a second family, in a way, since our brothers were so much older and not able to involve us in their activities. So Kim and I were constant companions growing up, and though we had our fights, they never lasted long. Archie comics were fun to read on camping trips in the tent or tent trailer, as we drove by car to Manitoba to see Uncle Bert and our grandfather, Dr. Fred Bird in Manitoba. We read all about Betty and Veronica and Jughead and

Reggie and never tired of them. In Boissevain with grandpa we'd walk down to Pringle's drugstore and buy the latest issues, and then head back to 710 Stephen St. to read them in that big old house or in the tent trailer set up in the driveway.

My friends used to say I had an advantage in school because my Dad was a teacher. I think they were right, but not because he gave me extra help at home, which he didn't. The advantage was all the books he'd had to buy to *become* a teacher, and which I had access to.

There was almost no homework in my day, in the 1960s and 70s, until about Grade 8. We had time to play after school and have fun. We were fit from all our running, and so you rarely saw a fat kid. Our imaginations had lots of room to blossom. Outside, we made our own fun with go-carts or guns made from hockey sticks, or 500-up (baseball) or road hockey and the like. Our imaginations ran wild. They ran wild inside, too, because our parents gave us a world of books, which opened up the promise and possibilities of travel.

For this, and many other blessings they conferred, I say thanks.

Chapter 2

School Daze

I WASN'T A VERY good student in high school. I couldn't figure out what the teachers wanted, and I didn't bother going in after hours to ask them. I ended up with an average of 76 or so, which was just enough to get me into Brandon University. High School was Prince Edward Collegiate Institute in Picton, Prince Edward County, east of Toronto.

We lived at East Lake in the country, near Cherry Valley, after all those years in the city, and let me tell you it was a change.

The other kids weren't keen to accept outsiders like my sister Kim (who was three years younger) and myself. This was a good thing to learn early, that you had to work at making friends. I didn't work at it, not then, and had few friends in high school. I joined the debating team and did well there, but that was about it.

Our English teacher, George Elson, announced one morning over the PA system that I'd won an award in a provincial debating tournament at Queen's University. Elson helped coach the team. But as he made the announcement I felt uncomfortable and put my head down in my arms on the desk. After being a good student at Elia Junior High and Stilecroft Drive Public School I wasn't much of anything at PECI, and this burst of fame bothered me. It was out of character. I was in track and field there also but didn't do much, though I'd been a good javelin thrower and long jumper at Elia.

The one thing I clearly recall from Mr. Elson's many classes was this: Mankind has a lot of knowledge, but we lack the wisdom to use it well. He wanted us to remember that, and to drive it home he taught Nevil Shute's *On The Beach*, a story about the last people to survive a nuclear war. A theme of this book was just that, mankind's inability to use its knowledge with sufficient wisdom to keep from destroying itself. But Shute, a great traveler in his own right, leavened the lesson with characters who also reveal the common person's innate nobility and good sense. I've since become a great fan of Shute's works and highly recommend his books. I especially like *Pied Piper, A Town Like Alice and Trustee of the Toolroom,* in addition to *On The Beach.*

When it came to selecting courses at Brandon University I had no idea. Dad suggested an Arts degree with a variety of things such as history and psychology and political science, so that's what I signed up for. I had no idea what I wanted to do for a living and that made it tough to know what to study. But career ideas would come in time, I was told; what mattered was to get exposure to information and people. I was 19 when I started at Brandon University in 1978 and for the first year lived in residence at McMaster Hall, a coed dormitory.

My roommate was Don Parent, a good photographer who was in his second year on campus. Don was an intelligent guy who spent a lot of time at the student newspaper, The Quill. He loved to take pictures and develop the films in the darkroom, as we did in those days. Don spent more time with photography than he did with his classes, I suspect.

"Do you like to write?" he asked me one day. Well, I'd written some teenage poetry and of course school essays when required. Yeah, I said, I liked to write.

"Why don't you come to a Quill meeting and try your hand at reporting," he said. So I did.

Before long I was writing news for the Quill. The editor was James Ritchie, with Beverly Neufeld his assistant. They were a good team. James was a slim, elfish man with a red beard and John Lennon-type glasses. Ritchie had a sharp intellect, a wry sense of humour and an infectious laugh, a deep nasal guffaw that you had to like. It often made me laugh. He was big on paperwork and procedure and once told me that "every bureaucracy ran on paper," so that's the way to deal with it. We of course at the Quill were confronted by BU's bureaucracy, and James knew his way around it. Neufeld was a gentle pretty girl, a Mennonite girl, calm and reassuring like a sister. She had kind eyes and a sweet way about her, and she taught me some of the basics of news writing such as how to hook your reader and then follow with the relevant facts and quotes.

It was the three of them, Don, James and Bev, who got me going in news. I'm thankful to Don Parent especially, because without his encouragement I don't know that I ever would have joined the paper.

I'd delivered the Toronto Daily Star as a boy, as had my brothers, but for some reason never saw myself as a reporter until Don mentioned it. I've had three decades of fun and rewards in news, and it's been a great run.

As a newspaper delivery boy I saw some chilling photos and headlines about the Vietnam War. The one that stands out for me was that of the the naked girl running toward the camera after a napalm attack. That's forever etched in my memory. I saw that image on page one of The Toronto Daily Star in June, 1972, when I was 13. I read later that then-U.S. president Richard Nixon thought it was a fake. It wasn't.

Her name was Kim Phuc, and she and her family were running from their home village of Trang Bang in South Vietnam that day, June 8, 1972. A South Vietnamese plane had dropped a napalm bomb on their village, which had been occupied by North Vietnamese forces. As they ran, a South Vietnamese Air Force pilot, on the side the U.S. was helping, mistook the group for enemy soldiers and attacked. He killed two of Phuc's cousins and two others. It's one of the chief reasons I deplore war – the accidental killing and maiming of innocent people who wanted nothing to do with the conflict. In big wars, hundreds of thousands of people die this way. It still happens today, and it's a terrible waste of humanity. But I digress.

Associated Press photographer Nick Ut earned a Pulitzer Prize for his photograph, and it became one of the most haunting images of the Vietnam War. Phuc settled in Canada years later, and recalled that she was yelling "Too hot, too hot," as she ran. She hadn't been expected to survive her burns, but after many surgeries she recovered fully.

Delivering papers was a real job, and I took it seriously. I'd pick up my bundles at the corner of Grandravine Drive and Sentinel Street and take them home to our garage. There I'd cut the wire that held the 35 or so papers together and put them in my delivery cart which Dad had made. I still have the blue-handled pliers that I used back then. Once you got the wire cut you removed the protective paper that hid the front page.

I delivered my papers by walking and pulling or pushing my wooden cart up Hucknall and down Grandravine and into Ladyshot Crescent, then home. I did this every day after school and every Saturday for about three years. I liked having my own spending money.

Once, when Kim was helping me, she delivered to a house with two poodles. In those days we took the paper right to the door and put it between the glass/aluminum storm door and the wooden door, which every house had. Tossing it on the driveway simply wasn't done. After all, the customer was paying for this, about 70 cents a week. Kim had to go through a gate to drop off the paper and that's when the dogs got her. They bit her, and she was only about 10. Lots of crying, and I felt awful. I don't recall those dogs being a problem for me, or I'd have done that house myself. I think it was just bad luck that they happened to be out of the house when she walked up.

I had one other customer on Hucknall who gave me grief. He was the last one on my route, so he wouldn't get his paper until about 5 or 5:30 p.m. Until this day I'd never been bawled out by an adult before, other than my mother. He was waiting for me in the doorway on this dark winter day and let me have it. I just took his wrath, not having the energy or courage to do anything more. But he was the last customer. I couldn't get him the paper any earlier.

Christmas tips were good, usually $1. You could buy a pop in a six-ounce bottle for 12 cents, a chocolate bar for about the same, a loaf of bread for 30 cents (I used to fetch them from the Red & White store for Mom), and an Archie comic for 10 to 15 cents, a quarter for a big edition. So $1 meant a lot back then.

The moon walk was huge. The Star's headline was Man Walks On Moon, in huge type, with a grainy picture of astronaut Neil Armstrong in his bulky spacesuit stepping onto the barren moon from the moon buggy's ladder. It was July 21, 1969. Other big headlines involved the assassinations of Robert Kennedy and Martin Luther King. I didn't deliver all those papers but do recall the news. For show and tell one morning a girl in our Grade 3 class announced that "Martin Luther the king" had died, and when the teacher Mrs. Rothstein gently corrected her on the name some of us laughed self-importantly, as if we knew better. In fact most of us had also thought he was a king of some sort. One time for show and tell I brought in a piece of wood to which I'd glued the head, fins and skeleton of a rock bass. A dead fish, basically.

We'd been fishing at East Lake on the weekend and it seemed the thing to do.

But my newspaper delivery days were my first real exposure to newspapers and I have Bruce and Bob to thank for that, as I took over one or two of their old routes. I likely wouldn't have thought to find a paper route on my own, to be honest. I took what came in life, because what came along was usually good. I said yes to pretty well everything I knew to be good, and still do, as opposed to planning very much in advance. I plan a lot more now than I did then. With time in shorter supply, it seems the sensible thing to do. I find that if I don't, other people will fill my time for me, serving their needs or wants.

In my second or third year at Brandon University I became assistant editor of the Quill, and then editor in the fall of 1980. But trouble loomed, as I was trying to do too much. Instead of taking the summers off as most students did to work and get a rest, I studied through the spring and summer sessions. I earned money working at the Quill and my parents were paying the balance, with the understanding I'd pay them back later, which I did. But the steady studying took a toll.

Two professors I especially liked were Dr. M.V. Naidu in Political Science and Dr. W.N. Hargreaves-Mawdsley in History. They were great teachers and great people.

I was in the flow, and ultimately decided on a double major in those subjects for my degree. Naidu was inspiring. He was stocky and confident, with an easy smile and laugh. He'd been raised in India and had become a professor when only about 22, and was brilliant and ambitious in the sense of wanting to leave his mark in the area of peace research. For years he edited Peace Research journal and put out a good product, and maybe still does. I'd help him with the work of stapling, etc., on occasion. He suggested I might want to become a professor, because it was a good life, he said, independent. Hargreaves-Mawdsley was a brilliant Englishman who died suddenly of a heart attack in my third year. I put out a special edition in his memory almost single-handedly that spring. Everyone else on the paper had gone home for the summer. That was the spring of 1981, if I recall. Once I clashed with him in class. I complained about our European history text by H.A.L. Fisher. He didn't stand for that, and put me in my place pretty quick. I'd got lazy and wanted fast facts, whereas Fisher provided a textured examination of history which required more effort to read. Being in the news biz made me rush through my studies, but I did manage to make some As and Bs.

Once I started writing for the Quill in 1979 things just took off. I began taking more initiative because I had something I really liked to do. So one day I went down to the Brandon Sun and talked to the editorial page editor, a kind man, about possibly writing an article or two. He was open to this. I wrote about the GDP as a poor measure of progress, since it tallies the costs of a lot of things we'd just as soon not pay for, such as pollution cleanup. I wrote about nuclear bombs. On this topic I wrote a series of pieces about the Candu reactor and Canada's role in nuclear proliferation in India and elsewhere for the Prairie Messenger, a Catholic weekly out of Muenster, Saskatchewan. This job came along largely as a result of a relative of mine, Kay Findley, who was ready to retire as their local correspondent. She handed the mantle on to me, with the permission of the editor, a monk, and that job worked well. It also paid me a little cash, as did the Sun articles.

I realized fairly soon that newspaper work was what I enjoyed and wanted to do for a living. This was a huge discovery for a young man to make, a very welcome one, and it shaped my future decisions and life.

I also volunteered once a week at the Brandon Mental Health Centre on the geriatric ward. I enjoyed working with the elderly and got to know one lady in particular, Ada Anderson. Ada was very soft spoken and had long reddish hair and a gentle personality. She was slim and of medium height, with nice eyes. Ada spoke so softly and rapidly it was as if she was afraid or unable to speak normally. Ada was intelligent and I often wondered why she was there at all. I found out she'd been admitted at an early age because her mother's new husband saw her as an inconvenience, if what I was told was true. This kind of terrible thing happened decades ago, in the early 1900s.

Ada was about 70 when I met her. I started by helping with summer picnics but moved into bingo calling and then just visited Ida and her friend, Judy, who wore a football helmet to protect her during seizures. Ada came to see my visits as something special, because the nurses told me she would do her hair all nice and look forward to our chats. I told her about the things I was doing and she quietly shared her thoughts with me, one of them being that I would make a good Salvation Army chaplain. I smiled at this. We got along well.

Another thing I got involved in was the environmental movement. In 1979 I started a student group called Students Concerned About the Environment – SCATE. This involved movies I would order from a group in Ontario, Pollution Probe, a well- respected group. These movies about pollution and nuclear energy and other topics I would show in the TV room of McMaster Hall. I had about a dozen regulars. It wasn't all easy sailing, however. Once the PR guy for the Chalk River nuclear plant in Manitoba wrote to the editor of the Prairie Messenger to challenge my critical viewpoint, and I felt a need to respond. It all took time and energy, plus my course work, but I was feeling good about it all. I was somebody on campus and I was contributing.

Yes, trouble loomed in my third year at BU, 1980-81, as I took on the editor's post and more courses. I was burned out, and had to step down from the newspaper early into the fall. In fact I quit all my classes and spent the winter working and living at home. Joel Salaysay took over as editor. He was a cheerful and brilliant young man, a good friend too. Joel was an amazing young fellow from Singapore who would suddenly break into song, or recite witty quotations. He chummed with Eng Chong Lim.

Lim was my best friend at BU. Both had served for a year in their country's military and had stories about M16 rifles and such. Lim was stocky and and confident. Like Joel, Lim came from a good family in Singapore, where his father was in business. But he wanted to make it on his own, not ride on his father's success. He taught me an important thing about private enterprise: most business people are largely motivated not by greed, but by the thrill of forming a plan and bringing it to fruition. In those days we were quick to slam "greedy" capitalists for many of the world's woes, maybe too quick. Lim made me see that they put people to work, gave people opportunity, and all because they were self-starters who enjoyed the process of building companies. I've looked at entrepreneurs in a different light ever since.

Among my other friends of the day were Margo, whose last name I forget, and Brenda DeCourte. Brenda was a fine, beautiful girl with sparkling eyes. She'd grown up near Boissevain, and I always had a warm spot in my heart for her. Margo was quick-witted and a very good singer. Margo was also bold. We were in the cafeteria one day having lunch or supper when an older economics professor, Don Wheeler, was holding court. Dr. Wheeler was self-assured and pretty impressive, as he talked about some political subject. Margo piped up that "maybe you're being dogmatic."

"Dogmatic?" the prof said. "Dogmatic?! Of course I'm being dogmatic. I'm *paid* to be dogmatic!"

I'll never forget that. Margo, for once, had nothing to say in reply.

A year of working and resting did me a lot of good. I learned about men's fashions while selling clothes for Mr. Big and Tall in Winnipeg. I worked with a salesman there called Emile, a Metis man of medium build with a mustache. Emile was never at a loss for words. One day a rather large customer came in asking for a belt. Emile took his tape measure and wrapped it around the rotund fellow's considerable waist. Then he checked our belt selection. He turned to the man, looked him in the eye, and said: "I'm sorry, sir, but we are cannot accommodate your circumference." I'll never forget it. He kept a straight face and the poor man had no choice but to leave.

Another time he noticed that I was going to the bathroom fairly often, and commented that I was too thin. "You really want to keep that stuff inside you longer," he said. Another salesman there was named Hal, who wasn't as happy as Emile. He suggested I get out of the retail business. I was meant for other things, he said. The manager was a nice man who taught me the ropes but when I declined his offer of entering management, he let me go.

Then I got a job with the government's Children's Aid Society as a helper with a hyperactive eight year old. I picked him up at home, walked him to school and spent the day with him. Believe me that cured me of any illusions I had about becoming a teacher (or a father, for that matter). During the breaks in the lunch room the talk was too often childish and petty, in my opinion. And the boy I was looking after was a holy terror who would lash out and hit other children unprovoked. One time I put him in his room at home for a timeout. He took out the screen in his window and escaped. When the job ended in June they asked me to stay on but I declined.

In the fall of 1982 I was back at BU and finished my four-year degree the following spring. I kept to my studies this time and mostly stayed away from the paper. I was accepted into the MA Journalism program at the University of Western Ontario in London, which began in May 1983. It was a 12-month program with a lot of practical work but also a major research paper, the near equivalent of a thesis. Mine was about 80 pages long and called 'Images of the Indian in the Early Manitoba Press.' I examined all the editions of the Nor'Wester Newspaper, 1859-69, and concluded that the proprietors seemed to deliberately overstate the threat of "Indians," who we now call First Nations peoples, to the Red River Settlement, which became Winnipeg in 1873. (My father's people lived there as Metis.) The paper's apparent objective was to hurry along the annexation of the territory to Canada by exaggerating the Indian threat, hence all the reports about "heathen savages" and "marauding murderers." In fact they were quite spiritual and reasonable when dealt with fairly.

Besides the thesis, we did a lot of reporting. We were the last class to write on typewriters, by the way. I take this as a badge of distinction. I wrote all my essays and early news articles on typewriters and am convinced we became better writers for it. Our thinking was sharper on typewriters because changing things meant crumpling the paper and starting from scratch. Mistakes created work, so we limited our mistakes. Computers make editing and correcting errors so easy that sloppy thinking can easily creep in.

In early May I was walking on campus one day when who should I run into but my childhood friend, Luis Kay. Hey Luis! I learned that he was studying toward an MA in piano. As far back as Grade 6 the guy had been brilliant on the piano. Mark Davis and I would go to his house across the ravine and his mother would say, "You must be very quiet. Mr. Kay is downstairs painting." He was an artist, a Rembrandt type with a goatee. He painted like Rembrandt, too, beautiful portraits and landscapes. The Kays were Hungarian and had left home during the 1956 Soviet invasion and gone to South America for a while, before Canada.

Luis must have got his creative talent from his Dad. He was tall and slender like me and not particularly athletic, but man could he make those ivories sing. He was also a good artist. I asked him if he needed a place to stay, and he did. I had just rented a room with a woman named Gaie Haydon who lived on Cheapside Street near campus. She had another room to let and told me to tell any prospects I met. Luis took the room of course and we three got along great, and Luis and I graduated together.

Mark Timm and Kim Bolan were two of my classmates. Mark went over to Southeast Asia to freelance and caught on full time with a news agency there. He wrote me about life in Thailand and suggested I try it. The women, he said, were very welcoming of Canadian men, and very beautiful. I was tempted. But I'd caught on at the Winnipeg Free Press after graduation and didn't feel any pull to go to Asia. I belonged in Winnipeg.

Kim Bolan went on to a career with the Vancouver Sun and did well covering crime and other issues. She's also written a book, *Loss of Faith: How the Air-India Bombers Got Away With Murder*. One of our professors was Andy McFarlane, an old Telegram man. Andy was a newspaperman through and through. He was a cheerful fellow and of course an excellent newsman. One time he listened in while the broadcasting instructor asked me if I wanted a tape of my TV and radio news broadcasts. "No," I said.

"Why not?" she asked. "You have a good voice."

"Because I'm a newspaperman," I replied. The instructor left, and then I heard: "Good for you, Brad." It was Andy McFarlane, who I didn't realize was just behind me. I was just being honest, but I wonder if Andy put in a good word for me with the Winnipeg Free Press after that, because I was able to do my one-month internship with them and then was asked to join them full time, which I did.

I had ideas of becoming a foreign correspondent even then. It seemed to offer adventure and glamour and travel. Early in 1984 we did our internships, and I was lucky to go to the Free Press. Living at home again was good, and the work was fun. I worked for Ken Gray, editor of the Tempo section. Dave Haynes and Andy Blicq wrote for Ken, while Greg Bannister was in business and Larry Hill was on city side, later to be our man on Parliament Hill. He's now known as Lawrence Hill, the award-winning novelist. *The Book of Negroes* is one of his works.

One of the first stories I covered was the annual spring fair. I found the world's fattest man and smallest woman. It was becoming clear that people stories were my forte. But I also wrote about a chicken that played x's and o's and actually beat me. Then I wrote about an exhibit that police closed down because it was too weird, something about a deformed woman. That made page one above the banner, my first-ever page-one story in the Free Press. Murray Burt was managing editor at the time. On the rim was Paul Pihichyn. John Sullivan was there, and Pat Flynn. John Dafoe was in charge of the editorial page. My month went well, and I helped it along by taking work home and having it ready for next day. I enjoyed the big newsroom very much.

Back in London after our internships, we worked hard. I found myself tired and depressed about three-quarters through the degree and went to see Andy McFarlane to tell him my problem. He suggested I see a particular shrink, so I did. I walked into her office and she started asking questions about my parents and what they had done in my youth. She began to blame them for things which seemed ludicrous. I said "enough of this" and walked out, never to return. But the session did jolt me into realizing that I had to bear down and get the work done. I wasn't going to get any help from a shrink. Maybe that was the method of her madness. I did graduate.

Chapter 3

The Winnipeg Free Press

IT WAS EARLY May of 1984 when the phone rang in our St. Vital home. I'd been home for a few days from the University of Western Ontario's School of Journalism, where I'd finished my master's degree.

Dad answered the phone and called me over. "It's the Free Press!"

I ran up from the basement, thinking it could be good news.

"Hello?"

It was the assistant managing editor. The rest of it went something like this.

"Hi, Brad, have you found a job yet?"

"No, I haven't, actually."

"The reason I'm calling is to offer you one. How would you like to work for us?"

"I'd love to!"

(It was one of those moments you never forget.)

"Good," he said. "Ken Gray would like you in his department. We were pleased with your work in January. You did all right. When could you start?"

"As soon as you'd like."

"How about Monday at 9."

"I'll be there. Wow, this is great. Do you happen to know what would my pay be?"

"Well, let's take a look. First-year reporter ... just over $30,000."

"Super. I'll be in Monday!"

When I put the phone down dad was smiling from ear to ear. I was too, pleased that this chance had come along. I'd briefly toyed with the idea of accepting a job in Hay River, way out in the boonies, and had even flown there to see the situation.

"Now you're set," dad said. "You've got your basic salary and you're set." I'd rarely seen him so happy. Mom was pleased too, but it was as if she expected this.

It was the start of a good time for me, the realization of a dream. I'd wanted to work at a great daily newspaper and the Free Press, at 300 Carlton Street, was, at that time, the best in the West.

I started working there on May 12 of 1984, if I recall correctly. I was 26.

In those days the Free Press was the Old Lady of Carlton Street. It was downtown, a stone's throw from Portage Avenue, maybe eight blocks from Main Street. The new Air Canada building would go up across the street and Pantages Playhouse, a former vaudeville house, was now a restaurant half a block away. That's where Dave Haynes, Greg Bannister, me and other reporters went for a cool one (or two) most Fridays after work.

The exterior of the Free Press building was made of large sandstone blocks, a substantial building unlike the new glass and steel structures popping up around it. I would get off the bus on Portage Avenue near The Bay and walk across Portage, then down Carlton to the Free Press entrance. Often I saw editorial page editor John Dafoe on the same bus. His great uncle, John Wesley Dafoe, had been famous for his work as editor from 1901 to 1944. The Dafoe of my era was no slouch himself. He won National Newspaper Awards for editorial writing in 1984 and 1985. He also had a hand in a third, he once told me. I held him in awe. I never dared to sit beside him, though perhaps I should have.

At the Free Press building we went in a revolving door, got in an elevator and rode up to the fourth floor to reach the newsroom. There was no lock and no security guard when I was there. This old building, so steeped in tradition, is where I had the privilege of working for 30 wonderful months.

Ken Gray in the Tempo department was a young editor, maybe five years older than myself. I liked that, and he prided himself for being on the cutting edge of trends. And Ken was usually cheerful. He worked with Chuck Biggs, a quiet man who toiled beside him as the section's layout guru, always busy with his pencils and layout sheets. This was before page composition was done by computer.

Our lifestyle section used to be called the women's section. It included trendy features, entertainment such as theatre and ballet, TV news and columns, and stories about new books, among other things. The reporters included Doug Whiteway, an elegant writer;

Dave Haynes, another gifted writer with a real comical bent; Kevin Prokosh, who outlived us all at the Free Press; Andy Blicq, who went on to a successful CBC career; and reviewer-reporter Randal McIlroy, who went on to become managing editor of Pemmican Publications in Winnipeg. We also had a movie reviewer who went on to a job in California, Len Hlady, if I recall correctly. I was about the sixth reporter, making it a good-sized department. This was about 10 years before cutbacks hit the big papers across North America.

What I recall is very little pressure. We went in at 9 a.m., sometimes earlier, sat at our desks or chatted with colleagues for a bit, and then read the day's paper, taking special care to see how our stories were played. This typically took about an hour.

Then Ken would methodically, one by one, call for each of us to come up and visit. It would go something like this:

"So how are you this morning?"

"Oh, pretty well, Ken, and you?"

"Fine, thanks. Hey, I was looking at a Datsun 240Z yesterday. What do you think of that car?"

"I like it. Fast car. Good car."

"I'm still looking. Maybe I should save the money instead. Anyway, what have you got on today?"

"Well, I've got that W. O. Mitchell interview at 11. I'm finishing the feature about the mice-infested Royal Winnipeg Ballet (before they moved into new digs), just need a chat with Evelyn Hart. And I've got an appointment at 2 with that ballet teacher you wanted profiled, Madam Mireille Grandpierre."

"OK. Get me the Mitchell story and RWB thing for today if you can. I may hold the Mitchell piece but we'll see how things play. Can you do the Q and A column today too?"

"Sure, no problem.'"

"Go on and have a good one."

"Thanks!"

I'd leave and he'd call up Dave, Andy, Kevin or Doug.

We used to complain about Ken now and then, the way people grouse about their bosses. He wasn't a perfect boss but neither were we perfect reporters. For the most part my stories were well handled and well played, and I'm thankful for that. Looking back, I realize that Ken put out a good product, and he was a good editor for me.

One of my first tasks was the book beat, which at this time was a lot of fun for the simple reason that many fine authors were kicking around: Pierre Berton, Farley Mowat, June Callwood and others. I interviewed the known, the unknown, the famous and the infamous. I can tell you I enjoyed every one of those interviews, though some were easier than others, and some led to better stories than others. I seldom if ever used a tape recorder and mostly took shorthand notes. In J School at UWO we were taught a system called Stenoscript, which I still use.

Among my most difficult but humorous subjects was W. O. Mitchell, famous for *Who Has Seen the Wind* and *Jake and the Kid*. When I interviewed Mitchell in 1984 he was 69. The book he was promoting was *Since Daisy Creek*.

On the morning in question the phone on my desk rang. (We didn't have computers at our desks. They were at separate work stations scattered among the desks, and we shared them.)

"Hello, Brad?" said the girl in reception. "Your appointment is here."

"OK, I'll be there in a minute."

My desk was half-way across the newsroom. Sports was at the back, nearest the reception area, with Scott Taylor and crew. You could always hear Scott; he had a lot of energy, a big voice, and he wrote a darned good column. Up front was managing editor Murray Burt's office. The horseshoe-shaped rim sat nearby, where Paul Pihichyn, John Sullivan, city editor David Lee and others did their work. I sat near business reporter Greg Bannister, city reporter Barbara Aggerholm (now also an author, living in southern Ontario) and Laura Rance, an excellent reporter of agricultural news.

I got up from my desk, picked up notebook and pen, and headed toward the entrance near the elevator.

Beside the receptionist's desk stood Mitchell, tottering and a tad messy. With him was a smiling, somewhat tired-looking woman (the publisher's agent) wearing an apologetic look. It was her job (poor lady) to guide old W.O. around. Which would have been a lot like trying to herd a tom cat.

Mitchell's tie was loose at the neck and grossly stained. His shirt was soiled as well, with what might have been mustard. His sleeves were rolled up to the elbow. His billowing white hair was uncombed, and he teetered a little from side to side.

"Mr. Mitchell, good to meet you," I said, extending my hand.

He grabbed it and pulled me sharply toward him.

"Lisshen, buddy, I gotta take a pee," he said, two inches from my face. "Ish there a pisser nearby?"

"No problem," I said, a bit surprised. "Come with me." The washroom was just to our left, halfway to Mr. Burt's office, and I steered him there.

After that I chatted with the publisher's rep, a good-natured woman. She explained that they'd been on the train and things were, well, interesting.

"No need to explain," I said. Mitchell had a reputation to maintain.

Our interview was almost a total bust. I couldn't get much sense from the man. I honestly don't know if this was a put-on or the actual effects of weariness and alcohol. I suspect it was a bit of both. And the story I wrote was nothing much. But I'll never forget our meeting. Mitchell lived for many more years, passing away in Calgary at age 83 on Feb. 25, 1998.

Sometime later I interviewed Pierre Berton, and was warned that he could be a bit difficult. I really wasn't concerned, as my job, after all, was to interview them about their books, not judge their social skills. They didn't have to prove anything to me, so long as they talked.

Berton was a big man, both physically, intellectually and by reason of his output. He was 66 when I met him in 1986, at the peak of his abilities. By then he'd written about 40 books; and when he died at 84 in 2004 he'd authored an even 50. You have to hand it to him, the guy was prolific.

But he was also a family man, a father as concerned about his sons as any other dad. I met him at a hotel, I believe the Fort Garry, as he was the featured speaker at a luncheon held by the local historical society. Berton's latest book was *Vimy*, the story of how Canadian troops took that infamous hill in the First World War when others had failed. The effort supposedly helped Canada come of age.

When we met, Berton was dressed in a suit, and was unsmiling and preoccupied. I was preparing to start my interview when he asked, "How come *you're* working for the Free Press when my own son Paul can't break into newspapers?"

I was surprised and a little taken aback. The personal nature of it flummoxed me, but I said I'd completed a journalism degree and did my internship with the paper. He didn't know me from Adam, and what prompted his question, I believe now, was simply frustration. Berton went on to tell me he was disappointed that the media gatekeepers seemed to be holding it against Paul for having a "famous father."

I said something about how things would work out, that it sometimes just takes time – which is odd, since Berton had spent more years in papers than I'd been alive. He knew far more about life than I did. He just wasn't at ease, he seemed sad and out of sorts, and I felt sorry for him. Our interview wasn't memorable, as his heart wasn't in it. My story as a result was also highly forgettable.

It was night-and-day different with Farley Mowat. Mowat was friendly, cheerful and plucky. He made a person feel good. I felt like I was meeting a long-lost buddy.

Mowat's reason for stopping in Winnipeg was *Sea of Slaughter*, his latest in a long line of pro-Earth, anti-exploitation polemics, which had begun in 1956, when his classic *People of the Deer* came out, three years before I was born. We met at the Fort Garry Hotel in his room. A lot of authors liked it that way. They were spared exposure to Winnipeg weather (the prime book tour season was fall and early winter, in time for Christmas sales, but often brutally cold) and it was a quiet and private location where we wouldn't be interrupted.

I always felt a twinge of nervousness as I prepared to meet a man like Mowat. He was a celebrity, an icon like Berton whose name was a household word. He was as well known and respected then as David Suzuki is today, and a brilliant writer. I'd read many of his books, such as *The Dog Who Wouldn't Be, People of the Deer, Ordeal By Ice* and *Polar Passion*. In a way, I felt I already knew him.

As the door swung open after my tentative knock I saw an elfish man with dancing eyes, a mischievous grin and a fully welcoming demeanor. My nervousness slipped away as we shook hands and his friendliness won me over. I asked all kinds of questions about the book, which he said was an effort to alert people to the destruction of species happening along North America's eastern seaboard. It was too late for many, he said. Man simply has to harness his greed and take better care of the Earth and its creatures for his own good: this was his main thesis. If we didn't change soon, man himself would become extinct.

In contrast to my interview with Berton, which I don't recall well, I remember the Mowat interview clearly, as if we'd just done it yesterday. I think this is because my emotions were very much in play in a positive way; I felt good, and I lived it intensely.

When I was four, U.S. President John F. Kennedy was shot and killed on Nov. 22, 1963. I felt very sad, and recall seeing dad watching the TV news. "What's wrong?" I asked. "Oh, President Kennedy has been shot," dad said. "It's very sad." And it was. I think we're more inclined to remember something if we live it intensely and emotionally.

But back to Mowat. His message might seem familiar today, but it was breaking ground in the mid-1980s. Rachel Carson's *Silent Spring* had come out in the early 1960s and Barry Commoner's *The Closing Circle* was one of many influential works that followed in its wake in the 70s, but David Suzuki was just getting started and Mowat was the better-known name. Mowat's revelations seemed incredibly sad to me, given what we already knew, and he told me it was not a pleasant read. I never did read it.

When we finished our interview, Mowat and I left the room together. We entered the hallway and stepped onto the elevator for the ride to the ground floor. On the way the machine stopped and on came three big First Nations fellows. At about 5-5, Mowat was dwarfed by these men. I stood 6-2 and was able to meet a couple at eye level.

As the author greeted them, I watched their faces, where the light of recognition burned bright; they were pleased to be meeting a man who had championed their cause of native rights and environmental stewardship.

"How are you today, boys!" Mowat boomed in his spirited manner. He reminded me of a six-month-old Labrador puppy, all eager to throw himself into life and have fun.

They replied softly that they were OK, smiling now as they realized who was addressing them.

"And where are you off to?" Mowat asked.

One of them said they were attending meetings with the federal government about land claims and related issues.

"Give'em hell, boys!" he said.

And that's what I remember of my meeting with Farley Mowat.

I also interviewed Chris de Burgh, by phone from New York. His agent had contacted me a couple of weeks earlier and we'd set a time and date for our chat, as the crooner was coming to Winnipeg for a concert at the Arena.

I was looking forward to interviewing this pop icon and carefully wrote down the day and hour of our interview in my Day-Timer calendar book, which I'd been using since Brandon University days when Maurice Koschinsky, a BU staffer, had recommended it.

About a week later I was at my desk and working on whatever when the phone rang.

"Hello, Brad, this is Chris de Burgh!"

My heart sank. I wasn't ready for him. This was supposed to happen a week later!

"Mr. de Burgh, so good to hear from you." Meanwhile I had my calendar book out and realized what I'd done – marked the wrong day in the wrong week.

"Sir, I have to be honest. I've made a terrible mistake in my Day Timer. I thought you'd be calling a week from today. Please – can you give me 20 minutes and call me back?"

He wasn't impressed. He did that but the energy fell out of his voice and I never did win him back. The interview was flat as a pancake and the story little better. I didn't blame him. I'd screwed up, and he was a big star. Had that happened in recent years, I'd have been able to wing it and pull off a good interview. But not then. I was too green.

Andy Williams was just the way he seemed on his TV show – warm, happy, and easy going. We had listened to Williams' records at home while I was growing up and watched his TV show with the bear, which mom enjoyed. Like the Carol Burnett Show and Donny and Marie, the Andy Williams Show was a variety hour of funny skits and popular songs by the host and guest stars. He left you feeling good.

Talking to Williams had the same effect on me. He was down in Los Angeles and was coming up to do a favour for a Winnipeg friend of his who was holding a fundraising event.

I told Williams how much our family loved his TV show. Well, I guess that kind of adulation is good for a guy because he was kind with me and gave a good interview.

Grant MacEwan came to the Free Press building one year to promote his book *Anna-Marie*. This was a fictional-biography of Louis Riel's grandmother, Anna-Marie Lagimodiere. MacEwan was tall and rangy and fit even in his mid-70s. He had a warm strong face, and for some reason he and I hit it off pretty well. He was almost as highly respected a popular historian as Berton, though not quite. I loved his books, found them highly readable and interesting, and admired the man very much. He was lieutenant-governor of Alberta for a while and had sat on Calgary's city council where he'd earned a reputation as a careful manager of taxpayers' money.

I greeted MacEwan with a smile, shook his hand and told him my name.

"Bird?" he said. " Did you say Bird?

I told him I did.

"Are you descended from James Curtis Bird?"

"As matter of fact I am," I said.

"Well, young man," he said, "you've quite a pedigree! Birds played a significant role in the growth of this country."

I said I knew a little about it, though not as much as he did.

With that we struck up a bit of a friendship, and he and I corresponded for a couple of years. His letters were hand-written and down to earth. One time I asked him to suggest a basic procedure for writing a book and he gave me one, carefully considered. He died many years ago but if I could talk to him today I'd thank Grant MacEwan because I've since come out with five books and have others planned. Maybe that's why he took an interest in me -- he could see potential.

I wrote a good story about his book and all was well on that front. With some people, you just connect easily.

One person I didn't connect with well was Randy Bachman. The Guess Who star was a growly character the day I talked to him. He and another local son, Burton Cummings, were scheduled to appear together on stage in Winnipeg and they had had a falling out some time back, so this was a reunion.

That wasn't a problem. We talked in general about getting back together and what it would be like for him after a number of years, yada yada yada.

The stuff hit the fan when I broached the subject, Gordon Sinclair-like, of his finances.

"You're a fairly rich man, I would imagine, Mr. Bachman. Are you a millionaire?"

He didn't like the question.

"I made my money back in the days of the Guess Who," he growled, adding a few more comments.

To be fair that's about all he said on that front, but I took the hint and moved on to another subject. Bachman was a good interview.

It was in the subject's interest, after all, to *be* a good interview. As an agent of the Free Press I offered free publicity, free access to many thousands of potential ticket buyers, or book buyers, or concert goers. The smart ones recognized that and cut me some slack.

I wasn't a rock and roll fan and did not have encyclopedic knowledge of the era's great bands, though I did have books at the paper to help with background.

One musician who didn't even try to be interesting or friendly was Bruce Cockburn. I guess he thought he was famous enough, well known enough, and didn't need the Free Press to help him sell tickets. He behaved like a cold fish, to be frank.

My interview with Cockburn was a phoner, and to be fair I guess his agent had set up a number of these slots and he was likely itching to be in the studio or maybe anywhere else but on yet another call with an insufferable reporter. Whether he intended it or not, that's how he came across. And of course nothing special happened in our conversation or the resulting story, for that matter. Maybe today, being more experienced, I'd pull a chat like that out of the fire.

Don Harron, aka Charlie Farhquerson. Harron was a class act. Like MacEwan, you knew you had a person of quality before you. Harron was a handsome man, which is funny because he looked like such a bumpkin when portraying Charlie, who was seen on TV's Hee Haw and other shows from time to time. His wife, by the way, was Catherine McKinnon, who sang like an angel but never, for some reason, hit it big.

I forget why Harron was in town but we had a good interview. He was engaging and respectful and pleasant.

Another class act was Tommy Hunter. The Free Press sent me to Toronto one year to cover the CBC's fall release of its winter TV schedule. I needed to file at least a story a day, and Mr. Hunter was taping a show one night. I managed to get in. It was in an older studio with a large live audience.

Before the taping began, Hunter chatted with the crowd and then introduced a couple of important people, who drew applause. He caught me off guard when he said, "And we have another special guest with us tonight. I'd like you to give a very warm welcome to Brad Bird, a reporter with the Winnipeg Free Press! Brad's come all the way from Winnipeg to be with us tonight."

Sure, maybe he was buttering me up to help get himself a more positive story, but hey, it was a classy thing to do. Everyone likes to be recognized.

I remember seeing Wayne and Shuster in Toronto, and big Peter Gzowski, the former host of Morningside, though I didn't talk to any of them. Wish I had. Remember, I'm young. About 26. And a bit intimidated. You don't want to make a fool of yourself by fawning over people. You have to be cool. But sometimes it was hard.

I interviewed Jennifer Dale on that same junket. She was absolutely beautiful, jaw-dropping gorgeous, and I couldn't get over that. I was face to face with Dale in what I recall was a little restaurant, at a small table. She was starring in a new series called Love and Larcency, and her lovely face was looking right at me. She would have been 29, at the peak of her feminine charms. I didn't know it then, but a year later she was divorced. I'd never seen anyone so beautiful. I couldn't function properly. I couldn't think or ask questions properly.

Finally she asked me if I was OK. I said, "Well, yes and no. I have to tell you something. You are the most gorgeous woman I've ever seen."

She smiled. I can still see that great smile. I melted even more.

Things went better after that. She told me how she was in a scene in which the costar had to forcibly take her and kiss her. He didn't feel comfortable doing it. They had to reshoot the scene many times. What a friggin' lucky guy, I thought. I later married Karen Stewart, who looks a lot like Jennifer Dale. By the way, Jennifer's sister Cynthia married the CBC's Peter Mansbridge.

I interviewed Mansbridge once by phone. I was doing a story about Big Breaks. Mansbridge told me his break came when he was announcing planes at the little airport in Churchill, Manitoba, and a TV (or radio) guy heard him, liked his voice and offered him a job. He never looked back.

A quick note about the technology we used when reporting from Toronto. I wrote my stories on a little laptop computer, one of the first in use, which had to be plugged into a phone jack. I actually had to go out and knock on the door of a little house to use their phone jack to send my stories home. For some reason the hotel didn't have one that worked. Maybe five years earlier they had been using typewriters at the Free Press, and you would have phoned home and dictated your story. My MA journalism class at Western was the last year to use typewriters, in 1983-84.

The Free Press sent me to the University of Winnipeg to cover a speech by Izzy Asper, Leonard's father. Asper was a former leader of the Manitoba Liberal Party and and an entrepreneur who at the time hadn't yet made it big in the business world, but was on the cusp. He owned a Winnipeg TV station and a few other holdings.

The man oozed presence and confidence. His eyes were somewhat glazed for some reason and he didn't look at all healthy to me. But he had a magnetic personality and I found myself going up to him after his speech to introduce myself and shake his hand. He had that kind of effect on people.

k.d. Lang came to town about 1985. Haynes told us she was appearing at a smaller-type venue and this would likely be the last time we'd get a chance to see her that way because her rise was meteoric. So a bunch of us from the newsroom, including Kevin Prokosh, Doug Whiteway, Greg Bannister and myself, headed out one evening to see her show.

Well, we got to the venue and it was crazy. There were people all over the lobby and everyone seemed to be waiting for k.d. We had tickets of course and frankly I didn't know her from a hill of beans.

Suddenly there was commotion behind us and I turned to see this young woman, mid-20s, head down, dressed in a western-style frilly jacket walking towards us. I could have reached out and touched her. She strode past us and toward the stage and we all stood and listened as she blew us away with incredible vocals. She was in her rockabilly stage and it was pretty bizarre, but you could tell this gal had pipes that could blow the doors off the Winnipeg Arena. It was a memorable concert and I'll always be thankful to Dave and whoever else was behind our little junket.

Colin Jackson of Prairie Theatre Exchange was a cool dude. I liked him. Very approachable and down to earth. PTE was quite a happening little theatre company in those days and generated a lot of news. One time Colin and I and Haynes were chatting about something or other, and the topic turned to salaries. We asked Colin what he was making, and he said around $26,000 a year. He asked us what we were making. We told him about $34,000 a year. "Geez," he said, or words to that effect, "you've got me beat, and I'm an artistic director!"

Yup, those Winnipeg Free Press days were fun, interesting, and financially rewarding.

One of my first stories was about a talking crow. A farm couple north of Winnipeg, Will and Adele Frazer, had found this crow at the dump, after someone had clipped its wings. They took it home, and soon it was parroting Adele, who would shout to the kids, "Close the damn door! Were you born in a barn?" I heard the crow say these and other things. Ken Giglotti took a good photo of the bird on my shoulder.

But there were down times, too. I'll never forget the sad day the Space Shuttle Challenger exploded. It was January 28, 1986. I happened to be sitting on the outside of the rim writing a story at one of the computers there when I looked up to see Paul Pihichyn's face go from blank to shock. He stood up and said, "Holy shit, the Shuttle exploded!" Then he went off to tell the assistant ME, the same man who phoned to hire me. They trotted up the spiral steel staircase to the composing room and tore off the front page, which was about to go to press. I followed them.

It's my only "stop the presses" story. They say about 85 per cent of Americans were aware of the tragedy within the hour. Challenger exploded only 73 seconds after lift-off. All seven astronauts died, including teacher Christa McAuliffe. The incident was caused by a faulty O-ring seal which allowed hot, pressurized gas from within the solid rocket motor to get outside and reach a fuel tank. Sometimes, even our knowledge fails us.

Today, there doesn't seem to be as many characters in the entertainment world – or in the media world, for that matter. Eccentricity isn't as encouraged or tolerated as it used to be. One man in the Free Press newsroom was mentally challenged (only one?), but he spent years with us, doing various gopher chores. They finally had to let him go.

I remember Elman Guttormson and Marion Lepkin, copy editors at the time who were not eccentrics by any means. Elman had been a Liberal MLA from 1956 to 1969, and in 1962 he won a National Newspaper Award while serving in the legislature. When I knew him, Elman would call me up from time to time and say, "Hey Brad, I've only got a minute to get a headline for this story of yours. Help me, will ya?" He was good-natured, I wish I'd known about his accomplished past at the time. He never mentioned it.

Marion was also a class act. She taught me how to keep my stories moving along. At the start, I had a tendency to pad my pieces by putting in unnecessary quotes, figuring I was substantiating my story, but it was too much.

The Manitoba Historical Society lists Marion Hilletta Epton Lepkin among its Memorable Manitobans. Born in Brandon, Marion was an award-winning student who started at the Free Press at the age of 23 shortly after the Second World War, when it wasn't common for women to get hired in journalism. But Marion had a long career with the paper. She was a feature writer and news reporter, covering beats that included suburban affairs, education, Winnipeg city hall and the Manitoba legislature. She began her editing career as a junior sub-editor and worked through the ranks to become telegraph editor, chief copy editor, assistant city editor and Canadian news editor. After moving into entertainment in 1955, she wrote a weekly column of television criticism and made numerous appearances on radio and television shows. In 1961 she became editor of the *Saturday Free Press Radio-TV Guide*, editing stories, choosing photographs, writing headlines and cutlines and doing layout. She wrote radio news for the Free Press and for the

CBC and, while living in Los Angeles for 15 months, attended seminars on radio writing, acting and production.

After I'd left the Free Press, Marion offered to help me get a job in Toronto. I didn't take her up on it, and went up to The Pas instead to work for Murray Harvey at the Opasquia Times. Marion passed away May 1, 2009. Maybe I'm wrong, but reporters – the men, anyway, because they could get away with it – probably had more room for fun in her and Elman's era. Many drank. Some of them traveled with hobos and wrote about it, and came up with other corny ideas, bankrolled by their employers. They spent considerable time talking, among other things, in press clubs. Staffs were larger, though the pay was smaller. Things changed when newsrooms became unionized and paycheques ballooned. It's been the same in pro hockey: as the pay went up, some of the fun went out.

But I had a great time at the Free Press. The only reason I left was itchy feet. I just had to get overseas and do some serious wandering. The Free Press wasn't about to pay my way. If I wanted to be footloose and fancy free, I had to do it on my own nickel.

The next chapter jumps ahead to recent travels with my wife. If you'd care to continue the story after my Free Press days, see *My Dear Boy*, which looks at my work-related journeys through conflict zones in North Africa, Kosovo and Turkey.

This book is about leisure trips, so we'll jump ahead to England.

Chapter 4

Off to England

MY WIFE PEERED at me over her specs -- the doubtful look a lawyer gives a client who has just proposed a dubious course of action.

"You want to walk around England?" she repeated. "In the spring?"

It was May of 2007, a cold, wet and windy day in Parksville, British Columbia. Perhaps it wasn't the best time to propose such a holiday. Our five kids -- er, cats -- had left mud prints on the kitchen floor; raccoons were raiding our home through the cat door; carpenter ants were feasting on our soggy back deck and Karen's mother, Mary, and my father, Clayton, had just died. We were now parentless, but we had each other, having married a year and a half earlier. I felt we needed a change, a jolt of good cheer.

"Well," I said, "I thought that maybe we'd walk around England for a couple of weeks. You know, see the countryside. Maybe camp a bit."

"Camp -- in the tent? England is cold in the spring, you know."

My wife, lawyer Karen E. Stewart, knows England, having earned a law degree from Cambridge. She is also a very good sport. In hockey parlance, a real gamer.

When I suggested a year earlier that we head up-Island for our honeymoon to explore, camp and possibly fish a bit, she embraced the idea. We had a good two weeks checking out lakes near Campbell River and areas north, and wetting lines for rainbows. But that was in August. It was warm. And I'd booked two nights at a resort in Telegraph Cove to balance the bit about sleeping on the ground.

Remembering this, I shot a compromise across her bow. "Of course, we'd stop at a bed and breakfast whenever you wished. And I understand the pubs offer rooms and good grub. We'd never be far from a hot bath."

With the deal made, the game was on. We postponed the trip for a year, as we both had family matters to wrap up, with our parents passing away. England, in any case, was flooded out for a while.

On April 15 of 2008 we flew to Gatwick and caught a train to Oxford. Our first stop was my cousin Dorothy Pollard's home near Didcott, at Brightwell-cum-Sotwell in Wallingford. My mother and Dorothy had been the best of friends, cousins, and they corresponded like girls over the years.

Upon our arrival, Dorothy welcomed us warmly and provided superb hospitality, including visits to Henley on the Thames and a nearby pub for supper. In no time, we had adjusted to the eight-hour time difference.

From there we took the train to Bournemouth, on the south coast. My father was there as a young pilot in 1943. He'd been sent to Bournemouth with thousands of others to await a posting to an air base. I wanted to see where he'd been.

Bournemouth, of course, had grown since the war. A large city now, it sprawls away from the coast but still has charm. We pulled our bags and golf cart off the train -- the cart we pulled or pushed as a carry-all for our gear – and strode toward the sea wall, a mere 10 minutes away.

"What a beautiful sight, Brad," Karen said, as she looked out on the ocean from our vantage point high on the walkway. It was, too. You could almost see the great sailing ships that once plied the water there under Francis Drake and other captains.

Yes, we were in England, and if felt great – but it sure was a long way to Christchurch.

After three hours of walking east along a promenade we realized it was getting late in the day, so we hopped on another train to ease our way.

At Christchurch we began our search for the Avon Valley Trail, which snakes north toward Salisbury through some very pretty countryside. As a boy I'd heard about the beauty of rural England from my parents. Mom's people were from Driffield, near York, in Yorkshire up north. Derek Megginson, my second cousin, and his wife Trish, farm there.

Dad spoke about visiting Derek's mother Kath and her husband in the war. This was another reason for our trip: find and visit Mom's rellies for the first time. But first we had some walking to do. Near a creek or canal at Christchurch we found a field and some privacy along a hedge row and, since it was late in the day, we camped for the night.

The golf cart held our nylon tent, bags with clothes, and a few food items. Hauling rather than carrying these things saved us much strain. I can't imagine doing such a walk without a cart.

The tent proved to be a fine little home, and as we bundled into our sleeping bags, I think Karen was even beginning to warm up to the idea of this journey. We slept well our first night out.

Next morning, however, we faced a challenge. After breaking camp, we came to a creek. But Karen took it all in stride. "Off with the shoes and into the drink," she said, and then forded the creek, with me close behind.

Then our cart began to give us trouble. The weight of our gear was too much for it, as the axle was buckling at both wheels. If we didn't get it fixed quickly we'd have a breakdown. We needed an anvil, some tools, and a welder. As we walked along a street, concern growing in my mind, we saw a middle-aged fellow in his yard.

"Morning," I said. "Would you happen to have an anvil?"

"I don't, but what seems to be the trouble?" he asked.

"The axle on our cart is buckling. It needs to be straightened and reinforced. I'm Brad, and this is my wife, Karen. We're from Canada and are walking the Avon Valley Trail."

That's how we met Keith Brookes. While his wife, Marg, prepared some tea and sweets with Karen, Keith and I worked in their garage.

We straightened the axle but only temporarily. Keith had some old tent pegs which we jammed inside the hollow axle for support. But it became clear that what was really needed was a welded reinforcement bar to give the axle strength.

Sitting in their back room, we shared the early stages of our walk with the Brookeses, had a very nice visit, then thanked them for their help and headed on.

A few minutes farther along Ringwood Road, Karen cried out, "Look, Brad, a welder's shop!" It was called Sopley Forge. The owner, a man in his 50s named Dennis, told us he had 20 minutes left in his working day. It was Saturday at 12:10.

"Closing up soon," Dennis said -- but we appealed to him, and he had a good heart. It happened that he had an assistant who was also from Canada, so we had a bit of an "in."

Within minutes, Dennis had welded a bar on the axle. This wasn't a patch job but a permanent fix.

"Dennis, that's great," I said. "We're so grateful. How much do we owe you?"

"Five pounds."

"That's all?"

Five pounds was all he would accept. Our cart worries were over, at least for the moment.

Chapter 5

Kissing Horses in the New Forest

FEELING SO MUCH better, we walked over to Ringwood and spent the night at the original White Hart Inn. King Henry VII had stayed there in the 15th century and found an albino deer, or hart, while hunting, hence the name. We enjoyed a fine supper and warm bed and bath and already felt rejuvenated, such was the healing effect of the English countryside and its warm and friendly people.

The following day we walked along fields as green as any anywhere in the world, up gentle slopes covered in woods, along gurgling creeks and in the company of horses and cattle that roamed happy and free. This was the New Forest, really a very old forest, King Henry VIII's hunting ground, now owned by the National Trust, and it was as if we'd stepped back in time.

"The horses are coming for a visit," said Karen, and sure enough, two were on their way to see us. Fortunately we had carrots in our pockets, intended as snacks for ourselves but it isn't every day we got to feed horses.

"Aren't you a beauty," I said to one dark fellow. I offered half a carrot and he quickly picked that off my hand with his big soft lips. I offered another piece and it also disappeared. I think that feeding carrots to a horse is one of life's little and unheralded pleasures.

As the horse ate, I stroked his powerful neck and soft nose. He was very friendly, and so close that I, on an impulse, kissed his nose. I'm not ordinarily in the habit of kissing strange animals of any species, but this was just one of those moments.

Unknown to me, Karen had caught the moment on camera. I gave the horse another kiss, and he seemed to enjoy the attention. After a while I simply ran out of carrots, if not kisses. But Karen still had some, and so she took over the feeding, with a horse of her own.

About 3,000 New Forest ponies can be found wandering freely in the Forest and its surrounding area and have done so for many years. In recent years, however, the future of the breed has not looked so healthy. With plummeting prices, many ponies have been sold for meat. Canute's Forest Law confirms that wild horses were present in the New Forest as early as 1016. Although they may appear wild, they are in fact owned by the 400 or so commoners who have grazing rights.

We walked a little farther along and came to another old pub, where we sampled lemonade (honest). That evening we got lost. Blame the trail signs, I say. The trail is well-marked, though, and it was likely our fault. We likely just missed an arrow.

We came to a pleasant looking cottage and the lady who answered the door. Kaye was 88. She lived with her dog and cat (which had adopted her, she told us).

"We'll try to set you right," she said. Our goal was the campground called Sandy Balls at Fordingbridge. She gave us some advice and we set off again. The camp is named for the large sand and gravel outcrops left by the glaciers. Tenting kept our costs down, as this was 15 pounds compared to 69 at the White Hart.

But getting there was a chore, and we were tired after all the walking. "Do you know where the Sandy Balls Campground is?" I asked a woman whose path we crossed. She did, and it happened that she was Canadian. We chatted a while and it wasn't long before she offered to drive us there.

We loaded our cart into her car and she drove us a couple of miles to the campground.

It was a large facility that featured a central dining room area that offered a buffet that night. We filled our plates with roast beef and potatoes, gravy and vegetables, and enjoyed the warmth and pleasure of being inside.

"This is more like it," I said, famished after the day's activities.

Then we returned to our tent site, as rain threatened. Quickly we put up our home for the night and got things under cover. It was a typical campground, few trees, with sites along a roadway. Fortunately it never did rain that night, beyond a few sprinkles.

Next day, we walked some distance and then were able to catch a bus to the famous Stonehenge. Located on a cold, windswept hill, Stonehenge held our fascination for an hour. But it was cold and uncomfortable at that time of year.

People aren't sure who put the old stones there or why, but it made for an interesting change in routine. As one website says, Stonehenge is surely England's greatest national icon, symbolizing mystery, power and endurance. Its original purpose is unclear, but some have speculated that it was a temple made for the worship of ancient earth deities. It has been called an astronomical observatory for marking significant events on the prehistoric calendar. Others claim that it was a sacred site for the burial of high-ranking citizens from the societies of long ago.

The stones as they are today represent Stonehenge in ruin. About 2,000 BC, the first stone circle (which is now the inner circle), comprised of small bluestones, was set up but abandoned before completion. The stones used in that first circle are believed to be from the Prescelly Mountains, roughly 240 miles away, at the southwestern tip of Wales. The bluestones weigh up to four tons each and about 80 stones were used in all. Given the distance they had to travel, this presented quite a transportation problem.

Modern theories speculate that the stones were dragged by roller and sledge from the inland mountains to the headwaters of Milford Haven. There they were loaded onto rafts, barges or boats and sailed along the south coast of Wales, then up the Rivers Avon and Frome to a point near present-day Frome in Somerset.

From this point, so the theory goes, the stones were hauled overland, again, to a place near Warminster in Wiltshire, about six miles away. From there, it's back into the pool for a slow float down the River Wylye to Salisbury, then up the Salisbury Avon to West Amesbury, leaving only a short two-mile drag from West Amesbury to the Stonehenge site. The biting cold sweeping over the hillside chilled us to the bone, and we headed down to the bus for Salisbury. At Salisbury we took in the incredible Salisbury Cathedral, a mammoth structure. Being choralists, Karen and I took in the Evensong that evening. The men's and children's voices were angelic and truly left us feeling holy, thankful and humble.

Afterwards we looked upon one of only four copies of the Magna Carta, an unexpected bonus. As a student of political science, I had long hoped to see that document, which was signed in 1215 and serves as a foundation stone of our democratic rights. Karen, being a lawyer, was just as enthralled as I was.

From Salisbury we took the train north to York -- for more fun.

Chapter 6

England's Public Pathways

IN TERMS OF marked trails and scenic beauty, I don't know if there's a better place in the world than Great Britain for extended walks. At last count the right-of-way network totaled about 140,000 miles, or 225,000 kilometres, an incredible figure not even approximated in Canada or the United States. And many of the paths in England have existed for centuries. When my wife and I decided to walk in England's north, we had numerous trails to choose from. Some are well known, such as Hadrian's Wall Path, The Coast to Coast Walk, and The Dales Way. Others are less known or not even listed in our "Bible," the Lonely Planet's *Walking in Britain* guide. Among these was the Yorkshire Wolds Way.

This 79-mile or 127-kilometre walk starts at Hessle on the Humber River, beside one of the longest suspension bridges in the world, and ends up at Filey, a fishing town on the northeast coast. Of course you can stop shorter if you like, as we did.

We definitely benefited by choosing The Wolds Way, a path "less traveled," to use Robert Frost's words. Those of you graduating from high school or university might give it some thought, this idea of the path less traveled by. There can be merit but also risk attached to such a course, many of us have found. It might lead to something good, or to a dead end. You never know until you try.

The Wolds Way was closest to Driffield, our home base, making my relatives' job of dropping us off and picking us up easier. We finished at Huggate, only six miles from Eastburn House. The walk was also in country my ancestors lived in for centuries, giving me a glimpse of my past. And it afforded wonderful views and opportunities to meet good people.

Walking, like life itself, is about the people you meet. As Aristotle once said, a man able to live alone is either a beast or a god. People are political animals, he said -- beings who live in "polities," meaning cities and towns -- because we need others around us for food, protection and companionship. You'd be surprised how many people we met while walking in the course of a day. You'll read about many of them in the chapters to come.

At the top of this story I used the phrase "right of way." This deserves an explanation, as it bears significance as a legal principle. Right of way in England allows walkers to cross private land on paths open to the public.

Sometimes this means walking through a farmer's private yard, 10 feet from his or her home, opening and closing gates on the way, past sheep and cows (and sometimes bulls!). The deal is you can do this as long as you don't fiddle with anything.

Even though nearly all land in Britain is privately owned, the right of way cannot be overruled by the owner. It is a treasured legal right going back to ancient times when walking was how most people got around. A legal victory in February of 2010 only solidified this right, when a Crown court judge told a South Petherton landowner in Somerset to remove a gateway to his large estate because it blocked a public footpath. Mr. Justice Cranston said Brian Herrick must remove the barrier, which he'd erected in 2004, to the ire of local walkers. Herrick waged a six-year legal battle to save his eight-foot gates but lost, facing legal costs of at least $500,000 Canadian. Walker Peter Kidner, a member of the Ramblers, a walking organization, argued successfully to have the gates removed.

In Canada, the closest approximation to such trails I can think of are the thousands of kilometres of portages -- paths between lakes and rivers – in the boreal forest region once tramped by the Cree and Assiniboine, with canoes on their shoulders. But these are in areas of Crown lands now, and they are not easily accessible.

In 2005, when I walked and ran 1,000 miles in Manitoba to raise money for heart and stroke research, from the southern border to Churchill on Hudson Bay, I walked mainly on the shoulders of roads. British pathways include some of this but not much, as most of their narrow roads lack shoulders. British paths take you mostly alongside farmers' fields, through woods, near creeks and into villages and towns -- delightful!

Right of way makes you feel welcome, as do the many signs on these public paths. Right of way opens up an incredible number of walking opportunities in England, Scotland and Wales that simply do not exist in Canada or the U.S.

In short, I suggest you consider this affordable, pleasant and health-enhancing mode of transportation, the simple walk in the English countryside. You can be amply rewarded because, while the cities have certainly changed a great deal, England's rural areas retain their magical charm and appeal. Age isn't necessarily a barrier, though do be sensitive to your abilities. Karen and I were told of one young lady who walked the entire Wolds Way in five days to celebrate her 70th birthday. On the other hand, as you know, exercise occasionally causes folks to drop dead -- a bit of an inconvenience so far from home.

The Cotswolds and Isle of Wight are two other ideal regions for easy walking, with food and lodging close by. If you can do it, and if you have your doctor's OK, the best time for such a trip is now, as soon as possible. We don't know what the future holds, so it's good to act on these impulses as soon as we can.

In the next chapter I'll continue our own story.

Chapter 7

Trish and Derek Megginson

"DO YOU REALLY want to be out in this weather?" asked cousin Trish, as the rain pelted down in the morning of April 23rd.

"We'll be fine," I said, climbing out of her little Golf. "We're basically waterproof, and in any case it'll let up."

It was a cold day. Trish parked under a large suspension bridge which crosses the Humber River at Hessle, in East Yorkshire, giving us temporary relief from the rain as we placed our bags on our golf cart to best advantage. There was a trick to this. Weight over the wheels was best, but you needed a certain amount up front on the handle to make the thing balance.

Karen and I looked forward to another challenge. Three days with Trish and Derek Megginson at Eastburn House near Driffield had been delightful, and now we were ready for a 40-mile walk to Huggate. Our journey would follow the Yorkshire Wolds Way, which snakes north through farmland and villages toward Filey. Our immediate concern was the mud, which made pulling our cart less than easy. To our left, the wide and muddy looking Humber River flowed rapidly to the east. For a while we followed a stony shore, and then found a footpath of grass and mud that made things easier.

The Wolds Way (a wold is a hill) became England's 10th National Trail when created on October 2nd, 1982, after other routes such as the Pennine Way and the Cleveland Way. "I think it was all about its stunning landscape," said Malcolm Hodgson, the fellow responsible for the route's upkeep. "It's a very special area. It's the end of the chalk line in England that starts down in the south, so it's a very different landscape for the north here."

Chalk? Yes, remnants of dead plankton and other sea life, which piled up on the sea floor over 70 million years ago. Today the chalk hills remain. The White Cliffs of Dover are made of chalk. You can rub the stuff and make quite a mess, I found. The hills are about 600 feet high and form a crescent- or moon-shaped ridge all the way to Filey.

This would prove a more challenging walk than our first venture in the south, along the Avon Valley Trail.

Centuries ago the wolds region was barren, used only for sheep. Now, after liberal applications of manure, it is one of the most intensely farmed areas of England (a hint to farmers who apply soil-destroying oil-based fertilizers). The sheep are still there, but so are forests and fields of grain. Into this world we trudged.

After a while we left the muddy river and headed north toward the town of South Cave, in farm country, along grassy lanes and over rough fields, the rain pouring down, adding to the fun.

A few hours of this treatment and the cart began to balk. Finally the bolts holding the thing together at the wheels sheared off, almost simultaneously. We were stopped in our tracks.

Our eyes met. At least the rain had stopped.

"Let's see what we can do," I said hopefully, as Karen looked on in concern. We had planned to find a soft bed in Brantingham, but this plan was now in jeopardy.

With spare wire and a few grumbles I attacked the problem, and jerry-rigged the thing -- only to find it wouldn't work past another 10 feet. The problem with my "fix" was that you couldn't hold the handle up high enough to pull the cart.

Then Karen had a brainstorm, suggesting we straighten the heavier ends of a bungee cord and insert them into the bolt holes, to serve as temporary bolts. This worked well enough to get us going. By now it was after six p.m. and we were hungry.

Not far down the road we found the Triton pub near Brantingham. A friendly waitress spoke to us with such a strong Yorkshire accent that we could hardly make out a word she said. We ordered the special.

Then the manager came by. "Delicious pasta," I told him. "Listen, we're Canadians. We're on a long walk, and our blasted cart has broken down. Any chance you could scrounge up a bolt or two, say a quarter-inch by three inches?"

"Golly, it's good to hear Imperial measurements again!" he replied. "You wait here."

Ten minutes and one beer later we had one good bolt, which I secured to the cart. This at least would get us going. We needed two, but the others he provided didn't fit. Since the Triton had no beds, we headed off down the trail and into a richly forested area.

Experience has taught me to pack it in when you're tired, or when dusk is close. Few things are trickier than trying to travel in a canoe in the dark. I figured it wouldn't be fun walking with a bum cart in the dark, either.

"Let's camp," I suggested. Though Karen balked a bit, preferring a traditional bed, we put up the tent, hidden as best we could in a wood near a large open acreage and manor house. We had a comfortable outfit, a rain-proof outfit, and it made good sense to use it.

An hour later, snuggled in our bed, we heard snapping branches and a loud male voice: "Are you there?"

"We are," I replied, and awful thoughts of having to pack up and move in the dark came to mind. "Sorry to park without permission," I began, "but my wife and I are on a long walk and we've run into trouble with our cart. We're from Canada. We'll be away first thing in the morning if you'll let us stay."

Then we waited. What would it be? As the landowner he had every right to make us pack up and move. He didn't keep us waiting long. "OK," he said, "you can stay."

What a relief. I thanked him very much and we soon fell asleep.

Next day we headed out in good spirits, but aware that we needed to fix the cart properly. The day was dry and pleasant as we made our way along the trail, which took us to Mount Airy Farm. I've worked for a lot of farmers over the years and figured if Brit farmers were anything like Canadian ones, we'd come to the right place. You can't beat a farmer if what you need is reliable, practical assistance.

"Good morning," I said to a man near a garage not far away. "Would you happen to have any bolts? We need a bit of repair."

"Come on down and we'll have a look," said the big man. It turned out he had a great many bolts and nuts and a big heart too, for soon Glen May – that was his name – was down beside the cart inspecting the problem. In minutes he had us fixed up and in possession of spare bolts, too. No charge.

Our minds now at ease, we walked toward South Cave, smiling.

Chapter 8

Are You Fed Up?

THE SOUTH CAVE Takeaway, with its orange roof tiles and old-English ambiance, served up a pleasant breakfast of poached eggs, toast and tea for a couple of hungry Canadians the morning of Friday, April 25th.

"We're a regular stopping point for people walking," said server Gaynor Edson, who was also its owner. "They come from the south, from London, from Europe. I'm aware of a 70-year-old lady, that's what she did for her 70th birthday, she walked the whole way. So when you feel tired, think of her!"

My wife Karen and I were into our second day of walking the Yorkshire Wolds Way. Rather than tired, we now felt energized. There's nothing like a cup of tea and a bit of food to make the world seem like heaven itself.

A book called *Walking Holidays in the Wolds*, lying on a nearby table, noted: "It's a delight to discover the peace and tranquility of the wolds, where you'll mainly be on your own, except for sheep and skylarks."

This we found was true as sheep, birds, grass, more sheep, small sheep, big sheep, dirty sheep, bold sheep and skittish sheep stood out as the more common feature of this route. At one point, Karen and I even resorted to picking sheep's wool off the ground, we found it in such fluffy abundance. This we washed and kept as souvenirs.

But no, I made no attempt to kiss a sheep. Horses are more cooperative. Prettier, too. Cats, with their soft furry heads, are even better.

"Let's pick up some cold meats and things and make a picnic lunch," Karen suggested, so we headed off in search of a store. Round the corner was a butcher who had just what we needed, and we stocked up enough for two days, including fruit and bread.

The village of Market Weighton, near Goodmanham, seemed a good destination for the day, as there were a couple of bed and breakfasts in the area and we were due for a bath or shower. On my own, I'd have stripped down and bathed in a creek, but a man must show some decorum when the wife is present and involved.

We walked on and on, over hill and dale, through stiles and farmyards and fields, past sheep and sprouting grains, rarely seeing another human being. Maybe indeed this is what heaven is like.

Stiles were new to us. These are steps used for crossing a fence. Stiles posed challenges, as we had to pull our bags off the cart and pass them over the fence, followed by the cart and ourselves, but we became adept at this.

At one point two mallard drakes flew in and landed awkwardly on the dirt a few metres away, apparently wanting us to feed them. We laughed at this sight, snapped a couple of photos and walked on, telling them how silly they were.

As the afternoon wore on we discovered to our growing dismay that we were apparently lost. Market Weighton was the goal, but our trail didn't take us there. Somehow we'd missed a turn.

Down a lane we strode toward a farmhouse. "You look exhausted," the lady said at her door. She exuded sympathy and tried to tell us how to get to the village.

"Are you fed up?" she asked.

We nodded.

"Would you like me to drive you there?"

We nodded vigorously.

"Load your things in my car, then."

We followed her lead, and she even phoned ahead to a B&B for a booking, but it was full. The next one: "Yes, one room left."

Five minutes later we pulled into the lane of an old farmhouse called Towthorpe Grange. It was owned by Penelope Rowlands, a friendly and soft spoken woman of about 55 who wore a dress. Penelope bred buff Orpington chickens, an old-fashioned breed of large, colourful birds named after Orpington, England. As a breed they're too big to fly, but produce lots of meat. They're good backyard birds.

She told us one visitor from the city asked her, "Is that a chicken?" She had never seen a chicken before.

For us, Penelope, her chickens and her room for rent were just what the doctor ordered. We hauled the buggy out of the weather and pulled off the bags we needed, and then headed upstairs to our home for the night. It was a lovely room, with two windows and a bathroom close by. We soaked ourselves in hot soapy water and then got out our food for a bit of supper.

"Good thing we stopped at that butcher shop," I said, as Karen cut into some sausage and I got out the bread. It was a simple meal but so very tasty and well deserved, after the day's walk. We ate it on the bed, as there was no other place to do so.

It's quite incredible how a comfortable room can seem like home after a good day's walk. We luxuriated in it all, reading our novels and relaxing before going to sleep. All was quiet, except for a cluck or two from outside.

Next day, Penelope provided a lovely and classic English breakfast, with fine linen and silverware.

Luckily for us the Wolds Way passed through her yard, making for an easy start. We headed out for another day of fresh air and fun.

Chapter 9

The Wolds Way

IT WAS NOW Saturday, April 26, and we'd flown out of Vancouver on the 15th, 12

days earlier. Karen had five days remaining in England, I had 10. It felt like we had already been away a long time, a satisfying time, and we already felt refreshed and rejuvenated. It was sweet to know we had more time in this beautiful country.

The day was breezy, cool and partly cloudy as we headed north on a grassy lane from Towthorpe Grange toward Huggate. Half an hour into our walk we saw two young people with backpacks only 100 yards or so ahead, who had come in from another path. I called out a greeting hoping they might be going our way.

They were. Paul and Cathy were on holiday from Leeds, a city of 750,000 in West Yorkshire, and they knew a lot about The Wolds Way.

"Apparently the scenery gets progressively better as you go along," said Paul, who was about 30. The environment was of more than passing interest to these two because they worked for the government's Environment ministry. For some time they had worked together in an investigative branch which did covert operations, hiding among the bushes and the like to spy on companies sometimes found to be breaking laws. Paul clearly loved his work, and spoke of occasions when they succeeded in protecting waterways and other natural areas.

Cathy, though, was less happy. When Paul marched ahead a bit, she told us she had accepted an offer to take on a new job in the ministry, and she didn't like it. Too many meetings. Not enough hands on. Little satisfaction and lots of regret. Karen and I listened as she explained; Cathy seemed glad to have sympathetic ears. Also at issue was their relationship. She wanted to get married but he did not, having been there and done that unhappily before.

This was a bit of a cloud on our sunny horizon.

"I don't know where our relationship is going," Cathy said.

Suddenly our fairy-tale holiday was hit with other people's problems. Thankfully we didn't have such problems. A feeling of gratitude welled up inside me and I turned to kiss Karen. I'd proposed three weeks after meeting her and we'd married after six months, no messing around. We had our moments like any couple, and at first the change to Parksville from Manitoba had been painful for me. I left behind friends, family, work and identity. There I was known and respected as a writer and park employee and chorus member, among other things.

In Parksville I was initially unknown -- the Invisible Man, a role I disliked, as I had achieved some success in Manitoba and enjoyed stopping and chatting with people.

In a small prairie town a trip to the store is a social occasion. You see people you know and stop and talk. Here, I'd walk into a store and see nobody I knew, and few knew me. Invisible.

It took two years to rebuild my life and adjust, to plug into Oceanside. In the process I learned that others have had much the same experience. Fortunately, Karen rode out my grumbling and discontent with forbearance and forgiveness.

"That was nice," she said of my kiss. Gotta do that more often, I thought. The four of us walked on together into increasingly steep terrain, through fields and woodlots. At one point the pathway opened up upon a valley, with a sharp climb up a steep hill. "This will be a challenge," Karen said.

Paul and Cathy, who carried packs, were able to ascend to the other side on a trail cut into the hill. We couldn't take that route, as it wasn't possible to pull the cart straight up. The hill was too steep, the cart too heavy.

Then I saw our chance – a sheep trail leading up at an angle toward the right, longer but much less steep. Animals always find a way. The cart was dandy on the flat, but difficult to pull uphill over rough ground. Karen and I trudged along, with her behind the cart pushing, and me pulling for all I was worth.

The hillside was so steep that the cart tipped over. I stopped and watched in alarm as our bags fell off and rolled. Karen grabbed and held what she could to set the cart upright. But it was a losing battle, as it tipped again and again.

We decided to stop and carry our bags up the hill separately. We were a little more than half way up. That worked, but it took a lot longer. At least this way we didn't lose or break anything. We'd had enough trouble with the cart and didn't need more.

Finally at the top, we looked around. We'd climbed a few hundred feet at least. I half expected Paul and Cathy to have gone ahead without us, but we found them waiting a short distance away.

"Bet that was a struggle," Paul said.

"It was, but together we got the job done," I said. "Straight up was no picnic for you, either."

He nodded.

Onward we walked, pleased by our little accomplishment and happy in the beauty of the day. For lunch, Paul and Cathy referred to their map and suggested a hilltop overlooking what we think was the town of Millington. Soon we got there, and it was one of the prettiest scenes of our English journeys. We ate our sandwiches in silence, soaking in the sun, the breeze, and the picturesque scene below, contented. Millington looked like a postcard.

And our friends seemed happier, which pleased us.

Chapter 10

Supper at Huggate

PULLING THE CART up hillsides and over fields was hard on it and hard on me. I was frazzled. When a smooth paved road to Huggate appeared, Karen and I jumped at it and left the bumpy old Wolds Way.

Birch and maple trees lined the narrow lanes. Once I caught a glimpse of a large weasel-like animal darting about on the ground.

As we arrived at Huggate, a village of about 300, quaint little houses lined the streets, and a couple of men were out washing their cars. There was no fast traffic, or anywhere near the volume of cars speeding through that you see in larger centres. Even Parksville, B.C., home to a lot of British ex-pats, is a lot noisier. Sometimes I wonder why so many British people leave home for Canada. The Britain we found was pretty and inviting, arguing strongly for home-grown people to stay put. But many have left, citing the rising cost of living in England and other drawbacks.

Paul and Cathy had booked a room at the Wolds Inn, the only hotel in town. Many old pubs have closed their doors in recent years because of declining business. It's a big issue, and one of the signs of a changing England.

"Rural life is unrecognizable from 20 years ago and British drinking habits have undergone a sea change as well," writes Michael Goldfarb in a March 2009 article in the *GlobalPost*. "Both of these factors have led to a crisis for British pubs. Thirty-nine a week are going out of business forever. And the bad news is accelerating. The numbers were awful before the recession kicked in, but now they are brutal. In the last quarter of 2008 sales of beer were off by almost 10 percent in pubs, according to figures from the British Beer and Pub Association. Now politicians are becoming alarmed about the future of an industry that employs upwards of half a million people."

In Parliament, the All-Party Parliamentary Beer Group has 400-plus members and lobbies the government on behalf of the pub trade. It was set up in 1992, according to Vice Chairman Nigel Evans, "to recognize the iconic status of real British ale." According to CAMRA (the Campaign for Real Ale) 2,000 pubs closed in 2008 with a loss of 20,000 jobs. A further 75,000 are at risk over the next five years if current trends continue.

Evans' greatest concern is the impact of pub closures on rural life. The majority of pubs going out of business are in country villages. "The local pub is more than a watering hole, it is the center of community life," the MP explained. That is true, agrees Goldfarb. "A good pub at its heart is an open living room for a village. It is not just a place to have a beer, but it is the place to organize activities, everything from outings for teenagers to the schedule of the local cricket team."

In many places, Evans pointed out, the pub is the last meeting place left for rural communities. Post offices are closing, rural bus networks never survived privatization, churches are closing for lack of worshipers, and schools are consolidating. Once the pub goes that's the end for most communities.

Goldfarb then looks at why the pub is threatened. "The flip side of this loss is that rural life has changed dramatically. In southern England within a few hours' drive of London, villages are empty for much of the week as the houses are mostly owned by professionals living in the big city who only come out for the weekend. Up and down the country, the automobile has liberated people from cities and suburbs and they can live in architecturally nostalgic havens a 45-minute drive from the office.

"Drinking habits have changed along with the shift in population. A stop at the village boozer is not an every-day requirement for the newcomers. They prefer to go to a gastro-pub: basically a restaurant in an olde pub setting with a chef who has been mentioned in the newspapers and a wine list to die for.

"Similarly, drinking habits in the cities have changed as well. For a decade and a half cheap flights to New York have introduced a generation to the pleasures of Lower East Side lounge life. Hip young Brits would just as soon go to a bar, flop onto a beat-up sofa and order a mojito or caipirinha as a pint of beer.

"Finally, supermarkets have begun pricing beer so low it makes going to a pub both an extravagance and for young people intent on getting drunk a waste of time. Some places are selling an eight-pack for 5 pounds (a little over $7), according to Evans. Compare that to the price of a pint, more than 3 pounds ($4.30) in many cities, and you can see what pubs are up against.

"Throw in the recent ban on smoking in pubs, which also encourages people to drink at home, mix it with an explosion in unemployment, meaning fewer folks can afford to go out every night, and the rate of pub closures is expected to continue to rise.

"Evans' group is pushing for changes in the tax code to help pubs be competitive on pricing. Currently one-third of the price of a pint is tax. As drinkers stay home, the tax take has diminished, so the government may reduce last year's double digit duty on the price of a pint in the hopes of luring people back to pubs.

"But even Evans acknowledges that there may be something aside from cost driving pubs to extinction — lifestyle changes among Britons themselves. An evening in with friends or alone, watching a video or hanging out in chatrooms online, with a can of beer in hand, is an increasingly popular way to spend time in this country. As Evans lamented: 'We're heading for a world where people will stare at each other on Skype and hold up a can of chemicals for the camera and call that socializing.'

The Wolds Inn had two rooms, we learned, and the other was also booked. When we arrived at the inn at 4:30 it was closed until 6:30. So we couldn't even get a beer. While we waited, I suggested we call my cousin Trish and invite her to join us for supper.

Trish liked the idea and made the six-mile drive in time for the meal, which turned out great for the five of us. This was the last we'd likely ever see of Paul and Cathy, and we said our good-byes. We'd enjoyed our day with them.

It was sad to think that our walks together were over, at least for now. Karen was flying home in a few days, while I had another week off. We'd greatly enjoyed our gallivanting around the British countryside on two major walking paths.

"So you liked the Wolds Way?" Trish asked, as we drove back to Eastburn House.

"It's a beautiful walk, Trish." She and Derek had done it years earlier. Next day, Sunday, Trish joined friends on a long walk herself, while Karen and I took Titch and Sprout for a run and then watched in wonder as a hail storm struck the area that evening. One thing about English weather, it's highly changeable.

Karen got on the computer and booked us train passage to London, as well as a budget hotel room and tickets to a musical, Cabaret, in London. On Monday we said farewell to Trish and Derek and hopped on the southbound train. In London we strolled in the rain and saw Big Ben, a statue of Winston Churchill (arguably the greatest human being of the 20th century painter, writer, politician, statesman, wartime leader. Yet according to a recent poll even many British youth don't know who he was). We also saw the Parliament Building and Buckingham Palace (both from a distance, as concrete barricades prevent closer viewing). A highlight of our London visit was a cruise on the River Thames. It was cold and rainy but we enjoyed ourselves nonetheless.

Cabaret that evening sparkled. The show left us in awe. Reviewers called it "brilliant" and "breathtaking" and it was. It appeared at the Lyric Theatre on Shaftesbury Avenue which was buzzing with humanity even at midnight. We stepped into a cafe and had a bite to eat, as the world raced by. It was thrilling to be amongst the throngs.

Our little room in the old Wellington Hotel was quiet. Outside, on Vincent Square, people played cricket. Next day we took the train down to Horley, because Karen would fly out of nearby Gatwick Airport next day. I wasn't feeling good about her leaving, but she had clients to assist. I had another week off.

Those last few days were a whirl of travel and sights and people. I much preferred the slower pace of our walks, and I think Karen did too. But London was a welcome bit of spice.

Chapter 11

The Gatwick Arms in Horley

As I ENTERED the little pub in Horley, looking for a cool one and a bit of company, little did I know what else I'd find.

It was April 30. I'd seen Karen off at the Gatwick Airport that morning, and with rain pouring down and fog rolling in I didn't much feel like going anywhere other than a suitable place for relaxing and drowning my imagined sorrows. One thing was for sure: I wanted no part of a bus, train or walking trail.

The Gatwick Arms, with its green and yellow exterior and four large flower boxes beneath welcoming windows, was quiet when I scouted it that afternoon. A few genteel men and women were sitting calmly over ales and discussing gardening and the like when I left about 4 o'clock.

When I returned about 8:30 it was transformed. Almost every seat was taken and the air was blue with expletives. What had I walked into, a mud wrestling contest?

No.

An NHL hockey game?

Close. A football match -- what Canadians call soccer -- brought to the screen by Sky Cable.

I'd stumbled into a do-or-die contest between Chelsea, a team based in nearby West London, and Liverpool, farther north, clearly not the favourite in little Horley.

"Drogba you clown, get the lead out and score!" came one of the few printable remarks, as tension built and the game's outcome remained uncertain.

I looked around, both to get my bearings and for help. "I'm a Canadian. What's with the game?" I put to an elderly gentleman to my right who appeared sufficiently calm and self-possessed.

"The winner plays for the championship in Moscow," he told me. "That's the European championship, and these two are the best in England."

"You folks get as excited about football as we do about hockey," I replied.

"You honestly care about ice hockey?" he asked.

I assured him we did.

Chelsea scored to make it 3-2 with only minutes remaining, and the decibel level soared. I regretted leaving my earplugs in my room.

"Take that you Liverpool sods!" screamed a man at the back at persons across the bar.

A boy about 10, sitting with his father at a table in front of me, scarcely blinked at this outburst. Nor did anyone else apparently find it out of character or out of line.

What concerned me was the brooding group of Liverpool supporters sitting on the other side of the pub. They were big and calm, like Mount St. Helens before it erupted. I had unwittingly pulled up a chair in the only space available, the no-man's land between the two camps.

The place was shaped like a capital H. I sat to the right of the crossbar. One leg of the H, to my right, was filled with Chelsea supporters; the other was occupied by Liverpool fans. The place was packed and space was at a premium -- and I held my breath while the Chelsea man continued to berate the visitors, egged on by his mates.

"Up yours, you Liverpool louts!"

"Yaahhh! Ha Ha Ha!"

We've all heard the stories of violence breaking out among British fans at football games, with fist fights and people getting stomped. This, after all, is the same spirited nation that held off the Nazi juggernaut in the summer and autumn of 1940 with a combination of wit, whiskey, Spitfires and spunk.

I could see the headline: "Canadian trampled in hair-raising Horley hullabaloo: 'I just wanted a beer!' he laments before expiring."

In the end, to the credit of the Liverpool contingent, peace was maintained. The game ended with a celebrated Chelsea victory. The man with the boy disappeared quickly into the night.

It dawned on me, as I drained my glass, that our passion for sport is really an effort to identify with a group and gain strength and purpose and meaning from something bigger than ourselves, both because we crave purpose (such as the quest for a sporting championship) and because we don't like to be alone. Which is the real reason I'd walked into the Gatwick Arms in the first place.

To probe a little deeper, being a fan often leads to disappointment. As a Toronto Maple Leafs supporter I know something of this. I think it's only when we use our God-given talents and "paddle our own canoe" that we find lasting meaning. Something inside of us has to be activated, and that requires work -- be it raising kids, helping the poor, building houses or whatever, depending on the person. Vicarious identification is not enough, which is maybe why the idle rich are often miserable. They're bored.

In eight days I'd be home and back to work myself. But first I had other plans for more fun in England.

Chapter 12

Ted Larkins

I'D HEARD ABOUT Ted Larkins from my father, who had piloted a Halifax bomber in 1944. Ted had been his flight engineer in the crew of seven, the man who monitored the engines and other aircraft systems, fixing them, or trying to fix them, when things went wrong.

Their crew survived 34 operations over occupied France and Germany, where they bombed factories, submarine installations, railway yards and cities such as Hamburg.

"A good sort," dad said about Ted. For dad, that was high praise. He said positive things about all six men, whom he regarded as brothers. Over the years, as dad declined, I'd been in contact with Ted, and we were on a first-name basis. He cried when I broke the news of dad's passing on Dec. 17, 2006.

Now, as I rode the bus from Horley to Poole on the south coast to meet him for the first time, I felt upbeat -- as if this was an idea the old man himself had put in my head. As much as anything, I wanted to know more of Ted's story. As my taxi pulled up to 6 Crib Close, a townhouse in Canford Heath in Poole, Dorset, I was a little nervous. What if we didn't get along? What if I didn't live up to Ted's memories of my father?

I knew Ted's legs were bothering him because he'd told me. But he was standing there with the door open when I arrived, 83 years old, with a warm, jowly face. "Welcome, Brad, come in, come in," he said. The eyes stood out too, lively and kind behind the wire frames. I grinned and shook his hand, and muttered something about how good it was to meet him. His manner put me at ease immediately. There would be no problems.

"Put your dolly round the back," Ted said cheerfully. "Good to see you, good to see you."

We sat and talked, drank a little beer, and watched the world snooker championship, won by Ronnie "The Rocket" O'Sullivan. Slowly, Ted's story came out. He'd been a boy of 15 when Prime Minister Neville

Chamberlain declared war against Germany on Sept. 3, 1939. He and his parents were living in Ramsgate, near Dover, on England's southeast coast, where Ted had left school to apprentice in the grocery business.

When things heated up at the time of Dunkirk in May of 1940, the coast was shelled regularly and at risk of invasion from Nazi forces which had recently overrun Holland and France. Ted's grandfather, a retired seaman, refused to move and remained there through the war, even after being injured by shelling.

Ted's mother had a sister in Wembley, northwest London, so the family moved there. Ted got a job in a factory and learned to use tools, which helped him later when he joined the Royal Air Force as a mechanic. Like his father, grandfather and great-grandfather before him, Ted's heart was with the navy. However, he'd already suffered one disappointment in this regard, when, at age 12, he was disqualified for naval training as a cadet, an inch short.

At 18 he passed the tests but was told the navy still couldn't take him. He was more urgently needed elsewhere. The RAF required men for air crews at this time, 1943. An officer advised him to apply as an aircraft mechanic if he wanted to get called up fast, which he did. Ted wanted to train on Stirlings, large bombers, but they were being phased out. Someone suggested he hook up with Halifaxes, but he requested Lancasters, and there was a spot open. As fate would have it Ted changed his mind, took the fellow's advice and trained on Halifax IIs instead. The Halley I and II were inferior planes, under-powered and flawed in design, and many young men perished in them while training or on operations (called ops).

The Halifax Mark III was a big improvement, faster and stronger, and it came on in 1943. "She climbed like a home-sick angel," dad used to say. To 10,000 feet it was faster than a Lancaster, whose turbo-chargers then kicked in. On high-speed evasive tactics like the corkscrew, a violent downward spin, it held together well and often enabled its crews to escape from search lights and ME 109s.

Early in 1943, Clayton Bird joined 18-year-old Ted Larkins and the rest of a crew which had lost its pilot. A bomber crew's initial operation was called a Nickel by Canadians (possibly because it wasn't worth a plugged nickel). On Nickels you carried and dropped not bombs but propaganda leaflets. Many men died doing so, because you were also a diversion to attract fighters away from the main bomber force.

During their Nickel, things happened. Two fighters attacked, evasive actions were taken, and the fighters broke off. Then they were coned in searchlights, blinding and powerful, freed eventually by violent corkscrew maneuvers. Their navigator froze from the strain, didn't have the right maps, and they were lost near Paris. A bit of luck and determination got them back to Blighty, shot up but safe.

After that, Bird's crew insisted he carry his lucky lighter on operations. It must have worked, because the only casualty was their plane, Daisy Mae, which took some hits from flak, bits of steel from explosives which narrowly missed the men. At one point, a piece ripped part of a leather glove off one of the gunner's hands, but didn't cut him.

Today, a model of Daisy Mae and a photo of her crew hang in the Qualicum Beach Legion 76.

It was terrible work, the bombing war, as German civilians and Allied airmen died in the thousands. But it helped to keep Hitler from replacing British democracy with Nazi tyranny.

Back from a raid, the crew would catch some zzzzzs, then pile into a little Opel car and drive to a pub for some ale and sometimes a supper provided by the owners, who took a shine to the boys. Practice took up most of their down time, however. Amidst the flying Ted also found love. During a leave his sister, Nina, introduced him to her friend Joan. Ted and Joan married and raised a daughter, Jan, who became a Baptist minister.

Joan died in 2005, and Ted has been alone ever since, missing her. I left next morning with mixed feelings, pledging to return with my wife, Karen, whom he wanted to meet.

"Thanks for everything, Ted. It's been a great visit."

"Come again, Brad. And bring that wife of yours next time."

"I will," I said.

Two years later I kept my word. Karen, Ted and I had a very good visit together.

A full account of Fl. Lieut. Bird's war-time experiences with Larkins and others is available in the book Nickel Trip, by Pemmican Publications of Winnipeg.

Chapter 13

The Shimmering Isle of Wight

As I PULLED the cart through Lymington's pleasant seaside core in search of a ferry to the Isle of Wight I began to feel again that sense of peace that comes from walking. Walking lifts the spirit and banishes the blues in quite a universal way. As Kevin Patterson writes in *The Water In Between*, "humans are most themselves and most at peace when they are walking steadily. Cities enervate and bore us. Hierarchies are the inventions of builders rather than wanderers, as are materialism and greed. Covetousness is a losing game when one already has enough to carry."

Patterson wrote as a sailor at sea, a traveler. My experience suggests that any sort of basic travel -- canoeing, walking, cycling -- works as a balm for the soul.

In his book, Patterson quotes writer Bruce Chatwin: Humanity's essential nature, he says, lies in motion, in nomadism and transience. "The further a people moves away from that original fact, the worse it is," an invitation to ill-health. Chatwin thinks it's no coincidence that so many today are ill in head, heart, body or spirit, given our sedentary lives.

Patterson agrees. "The most important thing was the tranquilizing act of putting one foot ahead of the other, and the ability to contemplate plainly one's independence from houses, from home," he writes. In this activity we return to the essence of ourselves, says Chatwin, and can understand our world and our place in it in a way forever denied a city-dweller.

Having walked together for 10 days, my wife Karen and I understood the primal satisfaction of long walks. Australian aborigines call them walkabouts. In Biblical times such journeys were a normal part of life, as people like John the Baptist hiked vast distances through what is now Turkey and the Holy Land. Jesus himself walked great distances. Can you imagine Him conducting His ministry as effectively from a plane or car?

Metis and Aboriginal people of North America trekked thousands of miles as late as the 1870s in pursuit of bison. They carried little and needed little. It's a matter of record that the first Europeans to encounter many of those bands described them as happy and fit. Turning from the wandering life to a sedentary one often broke their health as well as their hearts.

Until cars took root in our culture, walking continued as a common means of travel into the 1930s, when farmers either walked or drove a horse and buggy into town. They walked behind plow horses and oxen. The family car as a taxi service for kids didn't really begin until the 1970s or later. It certainly didn't function as such when I was a boy in the 1960s, when normally we were outside running and walking, engaged in fun and games. We walked to school, whereas so many today are bused or driven by parents, even those who could walk there in half an hour or less.

We walked to our ball games and didn't expect a ride, nor did we expect our parents to even show up. Parents, in our minds, had other things to do.

As an adult I've been happiest when on the move. Week-long canoe trips weren't enough, so I paddled across North America for weeks at a time. Day walks weren't enough, so I trekked the length of Manitoba, 1,600 kilometres, for three months in early 2005. Now, the Isle of Wight beckoned. But where was the ferry?

I found one without difficulty, and made my way across to the Emerald Isle. In time I made my way to Freshwater Bay, a village on the southwest coast. Two men stood on the beach, one of them dressed in a bright red wet suit. Near them, sitting in braces on the stony shore, fishing rods pointed out to sea.

"How's it going?" I ventured, pulling my loaded golf cart behind me. Piled on were my tent, sleeping bag, extra clothes and food. It was a chilly morning but a promising one. And I was intrigued by what they might catch. In every country it seems there are men like these, fishing from shore.

"Oh, slow at the moment," said the wet suit man, who introduced himself as Gary Edmonds. His brother Martin was only metres away, sitting now beside his rod, aimed like a spear into the air. Some 20 metres or so away their lines poked into the water, as the waves rolled in.

They were from Surrey, a county in southeast England. "We're only down here fishing for the weekend," said Gary, 42. They'd slept the night on the beach, in the open, and not too well, he added.

Gary, who was married, had been to Freshwater Bay with his wife and children two weeks earlier, but hadn't had time to fish. So he decided to return. The brothers worked together as builders. "He's a plasterer," Gary said. "I do suspended ceilings."

Then a fish hit. His pole bent. Gary grabbed the long implement out of its brace and began reeling in, suddenly animated.

Martin came over, keen on what they might land. After a short fight Gary landed a fish he called a ballan wrasse, and I took a picture. It resembled a big rock bass.

"Is it good eating?" I asked.

"Don't know," he said. "I've never eaten them."

"Too bony?" I ventured.

"Maybe, yeah," and then he released it. A good day for the fish, anyway.

I later did some research and learned the ballan wrasse is a common rough fish along the coast of countries around the North Sea. In the summer the wrasse seek shallow waters where they are easy to catch. The wrasse is a "regular visitor to my fishing nets" said one man on A fish blog.com when the nets are set in shallow water close to shore. The wrasse is also easy to catch by using a regular fishing rod. "You may then use a small fishing hook and bait it with periwinkles found in the shoreline," he writes. Most fishermen are not interested in the large and bony fish, but they can make for a fine meal, he says, and are easy to clean.

This was Gary and Martin's first time fishing at Freshwater Bay, a friendly little community on the altogether charming island known as Wight. The Isle of Wight is a world set apart, like B.C.'s Gulf Islands. It sits a few miles off the south coast of England, round and bite-sized like an English crumpet. Only 13 miles north to south and 23 miles wide, the Isle of Wight is eminently walkable, which is why I chose to go there for my last week in England.

For one thing it is uncrowded and largely rural, with only 133,000 permanent residents. For another the Isle has many miles of footpaths and 1,400 public rights of way, including a number of officially designated long-distance paths such as the Tennyson Trail. Poet Lord Alfred Tennyson lived there, as did Queen Victoria. The Isle's motto? "All this beauty is of God."

About 6,000 B.C. the island was part of the mainland, but the sea gradually encroached on the area as the ice sheets melted, producing Wight. Stone Age man was resident there, as was Bronze Age man, while the Romans left villas in Newport and Morton. Its name is thought to have come from 'wiht,' an ancient word meaning "lifted" – that is, from the sea. During their occupation of Britain the Romans named the island Vectis and built several villas there, according to Lonely Planet's *Walking in Britain*, perhaps because the mild climate and sea views reminded them of home It was early in May, time for me to hit the trail again and put the golf cart back to work. Two days earlier I'd said farewell to Ted Larkins in Poole, and hopped on a bus for Lymington.

A flea-market in Lymington offered up a heavy old pocket knife for four pounds, a good thing for cutting fruit, bread and cold sausage, which I lived on now to save money. The tent, hidden among trees, provided good sleeps.

I pulled out some cookies and offered some to Gary and Martin, who eagerly accepted.

"So what do you like to catch?" I asked.

"Pollock," Gary said, warming to the topic. "Sea bass, mackerel." They were using worms, but not ordinary worms.

"They bite," Gary said, showing me the pincers on the worms' front ends. I pulled back, having never seen biting worms before. They seemed like something out of The Twilight Zone.

We chatted some more and then I moved on, pleased to have had such pleasant contact with men who share a love of fishing (though I'm a lake man myself). Over the years my work has taken me to Morocco, Malta, Libya, Egypt, Turkey and elsewhere, and in each place I've always found fishermen by the sea. The ocean is a magnet, a balm, a source of basic food and relaxation, and lucky for me I would never be far from its waters in the week ahead. Luckier still, I suppose, is that Karen and I live near the Strait of Georgia and the Pacific Ocean.

Chapter 14

The Viking and his Gypsy Wife

It's NOT EVERY day you meet a Viking and a Gypsy in the same breath, but that happened to me on the Isle of Wight.

It's funny how it all began, really. After talking to fishermen Gary and Martin I'd struck off down the road and up through the Downland Walks Golf Course, looking to go inland to find some horses. I like horses, and don't see enough of them in my normal life in Parksville. Rural England was like a playground for me, with all its friendly quadrupeds to pet and talk to.

Animals rarely disappoint, and I find them good and pleasant company. I took great joy in cutting off handfuls of long grass and feeding them to horses of various colours and sizes. I spent much good time doing this. They were so appreciative, providing the occasional whinny and letting me scratch their gleaming necks and noses. Toss in the fresh air, the beauty of the landscape and the freedom I owned for one week more and you had a recipe for a healthy and happy man.

The best things in life really are free, though freedom itself has a price. This trip was costing me about $3,000.

On Wight I seldom glanced at a map, for it mattered little where I went or what time it was. On such a little spot of land, getting "lost" wasn't really an issue, and like a free-range horse I followed my nostrils and intuition.

From the lush pastures you couldn't see the sea. It was hidden by a ridge called the Afton Down, upon which the Tennyson Trail lay. The great poet loved nothing more than walking the vast green stretches along the cliffs, watching the interplay of birds, sky, ships and water. I shared his affection for this land, and came across the simple monument set up there in his honour.

I turned down Public Bridleway F61 because it felt like a good thing to do, and encountered other walkers who were there for the Island's annual walking festival. Then, up high to my left, over my shoulder, I caught sight of an old structure and felt the urge to steer my way there. It turned out to be the Parish Church of All Saints, the Anglican Church in Freshwater.

There I met the Viking and his Gypsy bride, and their dog, "Treacle." He caught my eye first, and appeared old and pampered, as all good pets should be. Black as the ace of spades, though dusted with the silvery gray of age, he sat happily panting in the arms of his mistress.

She was a striking woman. Sturdy, attractive, with a wide smile of gleaming white teeth and cascades of auburn hair, she exuded an energy you could almost touch. Her eyes were strong and penetrating.

"That's a cute dog," I offered lamely.

"He's a rescue dog," she replied. "He's blind. But he's got a really loving home now and he lives on a boat."

Treacle was tuckered out, having struggled up the same hill I had. Names were exchanged; I was talking to Sue Aston. But the man beside her was equally striking, tall with long white wavy hair and the same positive energy that told me, these folks are OK.

His name was Nigel, and he had Viking blood in his veins; he'd been living on boats since the age of 15. He'd served in the Royal Navy and had his own tug for a while. "I just have to be afloat," he said.

Sue, he noted, was an artist, a painter, and part Gypsy. They lived on their boat at Yarmouth, up the road a bit. "We live the simple way, we live our own way," she said. "We don't buy into society."

Nigel suggested we pause at the Red Lion pub a few feet away (yes, right beside the church) and we did, over ales and good conversation. Something possessed me to bring out the little photo album I carried of home, with pictures of my wife Karen Stewart and our cats and relatives.

I showed her a photo of Karen. "She's had some serious pain in her life, twice," Sue said. Indeed Karen's father and brother had passed away some years ago, wounds that could never fully heal.

"There's a child coming up in her life, in your life too, a disabled child I believe," she continued. Of this I had no inkling, and said so.

"She's a strong woman. And she sews well." Besides being a lawyer Karen is a seamstress, a skill she picked up from her mom. This went on in a similar vein, with a photo of my niece as well, and I realized Sue had rare intuitive abilities.

Then she told me a story. One day Sue felt a need to visit a particular town in northern England. She didn't know why, she just had to go. Nigel saw her off.

At the town she popped into a pub and sat. A man approached and said, "You're the one."

"I beg your pardon?" she said.

"You're the one who's going to help me understand all this," he said, and then proceeded to tell her a tale of woe about his wife. Sue listened and offered input. His mates interrupted to drag him away, but he said, "No, this lady's sortin' me out. Leave me be."

Some people are like that. And some days are like this one. Extra special.

Chapter 15

Christopher and Enya

THE TREE-LINED path to Yarmouth was pretty and sunny, mottled with shade, wide and smooth -- but choked with people. Cyclists with numbers on their backs sped by, part of a fund-raising effort I was told, and I encountered so many walkers -- ambitious souls with arms swinging – that I felt crowded.

For the first time in rural England I needed to get away from people. An exit presented itself, a grassy but muddy path across a field to my right. Pulling off to the side, I stopped and grabbed a sandwich out of my pack. I hadn't eaten anything during my chat with Sue and Nigel back at the Red Lion, so intent was I in getting their words down.

As I took a bite, a sandy-haired boy and a dark-haired girl pulled up beside me on their bikes. Both met my eyes. Then they looked over my cart and gear. Between us and the field proper was a large shallow puddle.

"Are you going down that path, mister?" asked the lad, looking toward the mud.

"I am, actually."

"We are too. Can we help?"

A kind gesture, I thought. He figured I'd have to unpack and move things piece by piece.

"That's good of you to offer," I said, "but I'll be OK."

I quickly stepped into a shallow part of the puddle and pulled my buggy through, its wide tires helping the cause. That went well and the boy and girl were pleased.

They followed and the boy pressed on with his discourse. "Did you make that buggy?"

"No, I bought it. But I did make a few changes to it, so that it could carry all these bags."

"It's very clever," he said. "You must be smart."

"I wouldn't say that," I said. "I'm just too lazy to carry all this stuff. You see, I have a tent here and sleeping bag so I can camp out, and that's more fun than using hotels."

(In hindsight, I wish I hadn't put myself down. I could simply have said, "Yes, it is a good little buggy.")

The girl, her eyes bright, liked the idea of camping: "That is splendid."

She and the lad insisted I tell them what each bag held, so I did, in detail which they requested. It took a couple of minutes.

Then we exchanged names. I honestly don't recall the last time I exchanged names with children. Do that in Canada and they'll have you before the courts on some trumped up charge. Kids in Canada, to their great loss, are taught to fear strangers.

I recall one time when I was editor of a newspaper and attending a school play to take pictures. I sat down in an empty seat not far from the front, with a woman on my left and a boy of about nine on my right. As we waited for the show to start the boy saw my camera and did what any curious boy would do: he asked me about it. I answered his questions in turn, briefly, assuming his mom or dad was sitting nearby. It turned out he had been left alone by his father, who was a teacher involved in the show.

After a minute or so his father came up to the boy, knelt in front of him, looked him in the eye and asked him if he was OK. The boy said yes. He asked him if he was comfortable there. The answer was yes.

I was not impressed. I spoke up, choosing my words judiciously. "Listen, mister, I'm Brad Bird, editor of the local newspaper. Your son asked me questions about the camera and my work. I showed him courtesy and respect by answering him. I don't appreciate your intimation that there's something wrong here."

He looked at me blankly, as if my words took moments to register. He said nothing in reply, and then left. The show started shortly after. I was glad I spoke up.

Most adults are good people. To bar children from talking to adults is just plain wrong. It cuts them off from potentially beneficial conversations. That boy might have pursued photography and done well because of something I said. Multiply that 10,000 times if more children spoke to strangers, because most people are kind and helpful toward others.

Kids aren't dumb, either. From dealing with peers and watching their own parents behave toward themselves and others, they know that human beings of any age can be dangerous.

It turned out that Christopher and his friend, Enya, were camping nearby with their parents. I let them steer the conversation as they wished. Having had no kids of my own, I was a bit out of my depth.

The boy wanted to know my job, so I told him, adding I was on the Isle of Wight to collect stories to write about later in newspaper articles and possibly a book.

"How old are you?" asked Enya.

"How old do you think I am?" I said.

"Thirty."

"Older."

"Forty."

"Older."

"Forty-four."

"Guess again."

"Forty-nine."

"Yes."

"That is old, you know," she said, her eyes locked on mine. I looked at her, all curly-haired and innocent and full of beans, and thought back to my own childhood days.

"And how old are we?" Christopher asked.

"You're 10," I said.

"Yes, I'm nine or 10, I forget which." (He was nine, but didn't want to tell me I was wrong.)

"And you, Enya? Twelve."

"No."

"Thirteen."

"Younger." It took me a bit to learn she was also nine.

"We went to France once and forgot the suitcase," said Christopher.

"Oh dear," I said. "How did you manage?"

"Well, Glen, my step-dad – he's not really my step-dad, mom's boyfriend – he rented skis and we bought a few things."

"I see."

"I bet you didn't forget anything," he said.

"You're right," I said. "Not this time."

"You have before?"

"Oh yes. Once I went camping with my father and forgot the tent. We had nothing to protect us from the mosquitoes. We were canoeing for two days. We slept on an island under the canoe, but mosquitoes pestered us all night. Do you have mosquitoes here?"

"Not many," he said. "Just a few."

We paused along the trail and I pointed out weasel holes, blue-bells and the like. One thing I had done was take children on nature walks when I worked as a park interpreter in Manitoba. Children love to learn about plants and animals.

"You'd make a good cub-scout," Christopher said.

We came to the end of the path and approached a road. "We have to go now," Enya said. "Please put us in your story, promise? You must promise!"

"I promise," I said.

Promise kept.

Chapter 16

'Movin' Day, is it Mate?'

THE SIGN APPEARED on a grassy lane on the Isle of Wight: "Please watch out for toads on the drive at night."

Touching, I thought, this concern for toads.

Next day, as I pulled my buggy along a paved road, a fellow stopped and expressed concern for me: "Need a ride?" asked the white-haired man.

"No, thanks, I'm fine," I said.

"Thought you might be having trouble."

"I'm actually walking by choice," I said. "A holiday. But thanks for asking."

He said something else, smiled, and then drove away. I figured I'd never see him again. But this was the Isle of Wight, for me a somewhat magical place, as you've already seen, where anything is possible.

To me it was a happy place of friendly children who talked to strangers, horses that enjoyed my attentions, clairvoyant Gypsies who told me insights about my wife, and lovely countryside where I could camp and sleep in peace. If there is a heaven, and I'm assured there is, it could do a lot worse than be like rural England, and this island in particular.

I had other remarks directed my way on Wight, all concerning my loaded buggy, a golf cart I'd picked up at the SOS Thrift Store in Parksville and altered to carry my bags. One day, while passing through the city of Carisbrooke, I passed a series of characters.

"Movin' day, is it mate?" one quipped.

"The missus give ya the boot?" teased another.

"Nice wheels, mate," said a third.

I smiled at each. Hey, unlike them, I'd been a free man for three weeks -- no phone to answer, no work to do, no schedule to keep. Free and happy and on holiday. For two of those sweet weeks my wife, Karen Stewart, had been along, making a fun time for us both.

Now, as my time in England ran down, I just wanted to savor every last hour. It was a happy time with the sun shining down and the early May air warm and breezy.

My thoughts turned to campsites. The first night, I'd put up the tent about two miles east of The Needles (an outcrop of rocks in the sea) in some scrub along the Tennyson Trail, near a mysterious circle of stones.

Another time I camped on the edge of a farmer's field near a muddy pathway, half a mile from the village of Wellow. It rained all night but I didn't care, warm and dry as I was in my portable home.

On this particular day I'd passed by Newbridge just after lunch, and had the encounter with the man in the car. A few hours later, at 5:30, I stopped at The Sun Inn for a bowl of soup and a beer. It seemed like a good idea.

I ate at the bar, as a bus full of tourists had invaded the place and taken the tables. The soup was good, the beer better, and I chatted a while with the bus driver.

Just as I was about to leave, a man at a table, a respectable-looking fellow who appeared to be in his 70s, smiled and said, "So, you made it this far."

He looked familiar. "You're the guy in the car!" I replied, smiling. "Yes, it's easy going. Good to see you again."

"If you don't mind, sit a minute and tell me about your journey."

I joined him at his table. "I'm here because of my father. He was a pilot in the war. My wife and I came over to see where he'd been. We also came over to see relatives I'd never met. My wife had to go home early for work, but I have an extra week."

He introduced himself as Colin Smith, 87, who was a war veteran himself and a water-colour artist. Some of his fine works, landscapes, adorned the walls of the Sun Inn, and were for sale, one of the reasons he was there. But he wanted to tell me about his own adventure, a 43-day crossing of the Atlantic from Halifax to England in a 20-foot boat he and his brother Stanley built in 1949.

"We enjoyed it, frankly," Smith said. They'd rigged a shelter on this small boat, endured all kinds of weather, and it was quite an adventure. Why did they do it?

As he says in the forward of their book Smiths At Sea, "Both Stan and I spent some time in Canada during the war (but not together) doing our RAF flying training in order to obtain our wings. We liked Canada and its people, so much that we decided to return as immigrants after the war."

In Nova Scotia they planned to go into the boat-building business. To make themselves and their boat-building abilities known, they decided to cross the Atlantic in one of their craft.

They made their boat in the basement of an old chapel in Halifax, and less than three months later the Nova Espero was ready to go. In early July, 1949, they headed out for home. The first few days were easy enough. Then the father of all storms struck.

"I have to confess I was a little worried," Stan wrote. But although things were uncomfortable and wet, his fears were unfounded. Sometimes the Nova Espero was completely buried under falling crests, but she never became dangerously filled with water.

The storm and breaking seas gave way to warm sunshine and dancing wavelets and all was bliss upon the smiling bosom of the ocean.

"The discomfort of living under the dinghy cabin-top became less acute. The confined space and the continual motion of the boat, which often threw us violently from one side to the other, ceased to annoy us. Nevertheless, the ceaseless motion did tend to exhaust us, and I have to admit to a feeling rather difficult to describe when my brother (Colin) bobbed his head down from the cockpit before dawn to tell me my watch was due."

They were not the only ones to receive unpleasant knocks, he relates. Once they fell from a crest onto a porpoise which didn't move quickly enough. There were many things to interest them, for the Atlantic is full of life. They saw many birds, and the only ones fighting each other were near the coasts. Spending a lot of their time in the Gulf Stream, they saw a lot of seaweed and other creatures including whales, which would approach to eye them closely.

One day Colin fell in – but his brother retrieved him. They sighted a dozen ships on the way across, and one told them: "Only a thousand miles left to go!" One day the crew of a French fishing boat gave them bread and onions and fish. In return they gave the fishermen a few sticks of black twist chewing tobacco.

Near Dartmouth, on August 18, 1949, they figured maybe a few friends would turn out for their arrival. At the sight of land, they finished their remaining run and were happy.

Large crowds in fact turned out, and they were welcomed home like heroes.

"By the time we sailed along the coast to Yarmouth in the Isle of Wight, our home, we had shriveled down to two tiny points of embarrassment, grinning sheepishly as we met the gazes of our old school friends and neighbours. If England was pleased to see us, we were overjoyed to see our dear old England."

And so the journey ended. The reception they got upon landing in Yarmouth was such "as to disrupt, and in my case rule out, a return to Canada."

In the war, Colin had wanted to be a fighter pilot. Most pilot trainees did, as that was the glory job. For Smith, like my father, it wasn't to be. He became an instructor, like Dad. Smith didn't like that much and they put him on light bombers but he saw no action.

He volunteered as a glider pilot and was sent to Rangoon in 1945, just as the war was ending. It was a good story and I wanted to hear more, but we both needed to move on. He invited me to stop in at his home, however.

Two days later I showed up at his door near Yarmouth, as requested, and we talked some more. He served a nice lunch and showed me his art studio, a cleverly renovated en suite.

His wife had passed on but he had two daughters, one of whom was walking in Sicily. We hit it off pretty well. Since I was going home the next day, sharing with Colin was a fine way to end the journey. He was the same age my father was when he passed away, and, like Dad, was thoughtful and creative, though dad's niche was music rather than painting.

That night I set up my tent on the waterfront, looking north across the channel. I was ready to go home. I'd been away long enough. It was time to get back to Karen, to our cats, and to my new job at the Oceanside Star, which would start May 12. It had been a wonderful trip.

Chapter 17

In Germany with Hannelori

"WHERE WOULD YOU like to go next?" I asked Karen during our English trip.

"Germany," said my wife. "Bavaria. I've got family there I haven't seen in 20 years, mom's people."

Bavaria, eh? I could see it: tall glasses of dark, full-bodied beer, smiling waitresses, walks in the Alps.

"Sounds good to me," I said.

"Without the golf cart, though," she added -- a painful concession on my part, as I enjoy bumming around the countryside.

"No cart this time?"

"No. We'll spend time with my cousins there instead."

I agreed. With one relative in a city north of Munich, and another south of there in the foothills of the Alps, there wouldn't much time for long-distance walking, if we wanted to spend a few days with each.

And so Karen and I made plans to spend 10 days in Bavaria in the spring of 2009, sans golf cart. Landing in Munich in late May, we were picked up by Hannelori Freitmeier, a second cousin to Karen who was close to her mother. After hugs and much happy chatter she whisked us north to Ingolstadt, a city of 120,000.

A retired teacher, Hannelori lives in a quiet neighbourhood not far from the city's core, which is a pedestrian-only zone. Ingolstadt is a pleasant old city and the home base of Audi AG, the car manufacturer. Like most residents there, Hannelori drives an Audi. The company gives them a cut price.

But in Europe, to varying degrees, cities have closed off their cores to cars except for emergency and municipal vehicles. We found it a vast improvement -- quieter, safer, greener, just far more pleasant. And the streets are usually filled with people walking and cycling. There is no shortage of shoppers. Many enjoy a coffee or tea on a tree-shaded boulevard.

We headed into the core next day and I managed to find a beer or two, and just sat and absorbed the view. At one point a boy and his mom stopped at a clothing store across the street. When she paused to look, he dragged her away, absolutely dragged her. I smiled.

There was no shortage of people or recycling bins. In Bavaria, recycling has been part of daily life for many years. We've just started to recycle kitchen scraps under a Regional District of Nanaimo program, but they have been doing it for at least a decade.

"After the war, people put their kitchen scraps out for the farmers to pick up and feed to the pigs," Hannelori told us. That went on for almost 50 years, until government deemed it unsafe and set up a program which denied the farmers the pig food but gave life to a new recycling effort. Today, very little is wasted in Bavaria, and landfills grow slowly.

And the place sure is green with pastures, wild flowers and cows.

Chapter 18

Fleeing the Bombing

IN CANADA, LITTLE has been written from the German people's point of view about the Allied bombing of Germany in the Second World War. It was a terrible part of the war that took tens of thousands of lives, both civilian and aircrew. Hannelori lived through the bombing as a child. I decided to interview her about that, and the following is based on our talk.

Hannelori Freitmeier was born Aug. 12, 1939, "nine months after her parents married," in Straubing, a town east of Munich. A few weeks later the war broke out.

Her parents were poor fur buyers. While her father stayed at home to prepare the pelts, her mother took them to Munich to sell. "They had nothing," Freitmeier said.

Her father was glad to give up the fur trade and work for Adolf Hitler, building roads for the Third Reich in the 1930s. A strong man, her father was pleased that a strong leader had emerged to put people back to work and restore German self-respect.

"He liked Hitler like a god. They all did," Freitmeier said. "They didn't know what happened to the Jewish people. I'm sure they didn't know... My father had been so poor. They believed what he said. They had nothing."

In 1944, the early successes of the Reich began to pale as the tide turned in favour of the Allies. The bombs began to fall in Freitmeier's area. She was five, and she had two younger sisters -- twins -- sometimes in her charge.

"We had to go in the cellar," she recalled. "One time we got a bomb in the neighbour's garden." The blast blew out their windows. Paper was used in their place.

"In the evening we could see lights. My mother would say, 'Munich is burning, Nuremburg is burning,' and we really could see it, an orange glow in the sky."

Her Opa and Oma, grandfather and grandmother, owned a grocery, where the children often spent the day. Oma had a big garden too, so they ate vegetables and bread but rarely meat, as the war dragged on.

"It seemed like every night the bombs fell. Later, they came during the day as well. That's why my father said to my mother, 'Go to Ortenburg'." His family, the Arnolds, lived there. It was spring of 1945, when Hannelori was six. But going there wasn't easy. For one thing, her father left to fight on the Russian front. For another, she said, it was forbidden to leave your home to flee the bombing. The SS were the police. "They didn't want to see that we had lost the war."

It also wasn't safe to travel by day. Freitmeier said she saw Allied fighter planes shoot people. So they traveled mostly by night. The trip to Ortenburg took three days in March 1945. "We left by bicycle. My mother had a child in front (on the handlebars, herself) and behind. We had a maid and she took another twin." They had more money by then. They laughed, despite the difficulties, because their mother was strong and capable, she said. "We three girls had white rabbit coats. We were rich! And she took the coats with her. We never wore them."

On the way they had trouble. It was difficult to cross the Danube River. They found a willing helper with a boat and crossed at night, again to avoid the SS and Allied attacks. "We had luck. My mother was so tough. She knew many things."

They were hungry, she recalls, and her mother gave them bread. As they traveled she saw no other people fleeing. Her mother had purchased a lot of cigarettes to barter for food, but the farmers did not want them so she traded a table cloth and related items instead.

When they finally reached her father's sister's home in Ortenburg, "the Arnold relative was not very kindly to us" because of the taboo about leaving home. But at least there was no bombing there.

Her father survived 12 years in the Third Reich's army. After the war he became a prisoner of U.S. troops, who denied him and his comrades food and water. He watched friends die.

"One after another died," she said. "That's the reason he didn't like American people." He refused to visit the U.S., where a brother lived. Freitmeier returned to Straubing in 1945, when the war ended, to find the streets filled with rubble, the old town destroyed. "There were only pieces of houses. In these, people had to live. And later there were rats. In Oma's house, in one room, lived five people."

* * *

A few words about this. It's important. One of the many tragedies of war is that it turns country against country and people against people, who might otherwise be friends. After the Second World War, airmen from Canada, my father among them, befriended former German pilots. During the war they tried to kill each other. Decades later they drank beer together at air force reunions. This is an example of people's tendency toward friendship and forgiveness, and shows how war is a rather fleeting state of insanity.

Walking in other countries can reduce the risk of international conflict by connecting us to other cultures at a very human level, allowing us to see how much we have in common. Most people seek peace; they work at having peaceful family and workplace relations; they apologize frequently and express forgiveness when necessary. Walking counters the culture of war by cutting through the crap we're told about "others" and revealing the truth: that most people are pretty nice and worthy of being our friends. Just as the German people were vilified in 1939 because of their leader, Arab people today are vilified because of a few violent zealots. It has been my experience in North Africa and elsewhere that most Arab people want nothing to do with terrorism and would happily welcome you into their home.

This is just one more reason to get out and start walking. Along the way it's easy to sow seeds of kindness and goodwill, because most of us are happy when we journey by foot. The endorphins are flowing and we feel good. Those seeds can bloom in positive ways, leading to happy results, long after we've departed for the Great Beyond. It's one of the best things we can do.

My 90-year-old uncle James Mackenzie Bird, who fought in the Second World War, says Canada is precious because people from all over the world can move here, live in relative peace, and speak their own languages as they wish. We do have a freer society than most. It *is* a special place. But I sometimes wonder what the young men who died in the war would say today if they came back to see what we've done with the Canada *they* knew. I think many would not be pleased. We have too many rules and regulations and too little respect for the democracy they died for, even among those in government. We maybe aren't as free as they thought we'd be.

About 60 million people, mostly civilians, died in the Second World War. Think of it: 60 million people, almost twice the current population of Canada, killed in one war. Many of them would have contributed much to the betterment of the human condition. Below are some examples of the totals.

The Soviet Union – 25 million deaths, only about a third combat related.
China – between 15 and 22 million deaths.
Poland – six million deaths including three million Jews, which are 20% of its prewar population.
Germany – four million soldiers and two million civilians.
Japan --1.2 million battle deaths, 1.4 million soldiers listed as missing, almost one million civilians killed in the bombing in 1944 and 1945.
Yugoslavia – over 1.7 million.
Greece – 500,000.
Great Britain – 324,000 including 264,000 soldiers and 60,000 civilians in bombing raids.
The United States – 292,000 soldiers.
Netherlands -- 200,000, including 10,000 soldiers and 190,000 civilians.
Australia – 23,000 men in combat.
Canada – 37,000 soldiers.
France – 600,000, including 200,000 soldiers and 400,000 civilians.

Yes, walking in foreign countries can help to prevent war and its many casualties. It can build bridges, foster friendships, and encourage respect for different ways of doing things. An example of the benefits of walking is Pierre Elliott Trudeau, who as a young man backpacked through India and much of Asia. He walked among different peoples and learned to value their ways of life. Later, as Canada's Prime Minister, he was opposed to war, nuclear weapons, and very much pro-peace. So let's get out there, our young people especially, and do more walking. Because peace sure beats the alternative!

In the next chapter, Karen and I visit a German city that was spared the bombing.

Chapter 19

Regal Regensburg

Lo AND BEHOLD, the German train system is human after all -- well, you know what I mean. Noted for their efficiency, Germany's trains are as susceptible to windblown trees as those of any other country. Karen and I discovered this while waiting for the 10:05 from Ingolstadt to Regensburg. Return fare for two was 33 Euros, about $50, quite reasonable. The 10:05 was cancelled but we caught the train an hour later and by noon arrived in beautiful Regensburg, noted for having been spared by the war. It was like walking into a museum.

The day was sunny and warm as we piled off the coach and into the busy modern station. Karen was eager to see some more old cathedrals, but I'd had my fill of churches and hoped to find a quiet bench (and a beer) by the water. I felt a little out of sorts, even though we'd been having a really good vacation.

Regensburg is the oldest city on the Danube, having been founded by Marcus Aurelius in 179 AD. One of the first things Karen and I saw was the ancient Stone Bridge with its 16 curving arches. This 1,000-foot long structure was built in the 12th century and is an amazing piece of medieval construction, the earliest bridge of its kind in the country.

It thronged with people even on this day, May 27, and I snapped a photo or two of Karen. Below it flowed the blue Danube, about as fast as the Englishman River near Parksville.

Once across, we decided to eat at the Gaststatte Spitalgarten (translation: "eat and drink here"), a restaurant by the riverbank under a canopy of large leafy trees, with plenty of tables and benches.

Nearby, under the bridge, we saw a large grassy area along the Danube that drew me like a bee to honey. Maybe it's a guy thing, but I got distracted. There were some old cottonwood trees of the type you see along the Mississippi River. We'd pounded so much pavement lately that I just had to go to the grass.

Oh, the Mississippi! I'd paddled that great river and camped along it like Huck Finn, not once but four or five times. Poor Karen got left behind as I strode to the trees, pulled along by an energy and intuition I can't explain. (Tell me, men, why do we do these things?)

All told I've spent about five months traveling the Mississippi in a canoe and they are among my happiest days. In 2003 I paddled it for a week with a friend. We returned to Winnipeg and I needed more, so I drove the seven hours back and spent another five days on its waters near Bemidji (I was working on my MA thesis at the time, but it could wait).

In 1991 Mark Bergen and I paddled from The Pas, Man., to Minneapolis and New Orleans, about 1900 miles total. One time we raced a paddle wheel boat in our underwear and overtook it, the people aboard cheering us on. Often we jumped in the river from the canoe and swam along for a mile or more before clambering back in, refreshed.

The riverside towns were full of used-book stores and interesting old-timers. Once we met a man on the dock at Hannibal, Missouri, who knew where Minot, North Dakota was, south of where we then lived. His boss had invited him to move up there and help start a new plant. "I'll do a lot for a friend," he drawled, "but I'd never live in Minot -- too cold!" We laughed. We were free, free, free! Oh, those were the days, in my early 30s.

Then a man with a dog shuffled by within feet of the river. I uttered a warning about the dog's safety and snapped back to reality. I looked around.

Where was Karen?

She was some distance away. I apologized for my absence. I felt good but repentant, like a disobedient pooch that had slipped the leash and gone for a run. The thing is, I love being with Karen, and I love Karen very much, but every now and then I need to be on my own. We returned to the beer garden for a great lunch, and talked and plotted our afternoon. All was well again.

Karen's guidebook took us to St. Peter's Cathedral. Then we walked into the Romanesque All Saints Chapel and discovered a boy's choir, the Regensburger Domspatzen, one of the finest in the land. We watched, very pleased, for half an hour while they practised.

We only had about five hours in the city but Regensburg was worth seeing, steeped in culture, and easy to walk around.

Chapter 20

On the Danube

"YOU WOULD LIKE the boat trip," said Hannelori.

"I don't know," I said, waffling. "We don't want to put you out." Would she really want to drive Karen and me to the dock, and then have to zip farther along to pick us up at the end?

"It's not a problem, and I'd enjoy the drive," she said.

"Let's do it, Brad," said Karen. "I would very much like the boat ride and so would you," she said, in that tone of voice I have come to respect.

It is good for a man to have a wife, if only so he can be reminded of what he does and does not like. We husbands can forget these things. And Karen was absolutely correct, I do enjoy river cruises.

We sat in Hannelori's home in Ingolstadt. She has a comfortable two-storey house with marble stairs and lovely old wooden dressers and a pretty perennial garden with shrubs and flowering plants. Hannelori had been close to Karen's late mother, and the bonds of family were strong between them. It did my heart good to hear them chatting and laughing.

It was late in May and Karen and I, with her cousin's help, were planning our next few days. We only had nine full days in Germany, so it made sense to make each one count.

"It is settled, then," said Hannelori, a retired teacher. "We shall go tomorrow."

Her own husband, Ernst, had died a few years earlier of cancer, and she missed him dearly. She said Ernst was a marvelous man. But, being alone, Hannelori had time for us, which made our visit extra special. Which was another miscalculation on my part: Hannelori truly wanted to spend the day with us and drive us around. It gave her great joy to share her beautiful homeland with us, as we'd already found out in a trip to Straubing, where Karen's mother's family lives.

Straubing was a blur of relatives, old churches, a great lunch and a funny story about a nunnery located across the street from a monastery, which we visited. Apparently an underground passageway linked the two buildings and provided the means for some extra-curricular trysts, which generated a love child or two. The elderly ladies with us shared this story with a smile and a wink.

Next day, on the way to the boat dock at Kelheim we stopped at Liberation Hall, an old monument on a hillside built in 1842 to commemorate the liberation of Germany from Napoleon. We went inside the large round structure and observed the large marble sculptures of angel-like beings. Climbing a narrow circular staircase we had a great view of the Danube and countryside. Back in the car we made our way to the river, which moved along at about five miles per hour, much like the Englishman at Parksville but wider and not so clear. The Danube picks up silt from the soil and, like Manitoba's Red River, is discoloured. Europe's second longest waterway after the Volga, the Danube starts in Germany's Black Forest as the smaller Brigach and Breg rivers which join at the German town Donaueschingen, after which it is known as the Danube and flows eastwards for some 2850 km (1771 miles), passing through four Central and Eastern European capitals before emptying into the Black Sea.

If you've been to Budapest in Hungary, you've seen the Danube. It's mentioned in the title of a famous waltz by Austrian composer Johann Strauss, An der schönen, blauen Donau (On the Beautiful Blue Danube). Strauss composed it while traveling down the river and it's well known as a lullaby.

Thankfully we didn't have to compose a song about it, just enjoy the view and the food aboard. At Kelheim the first thing Karen and I saw were ducks -- not in the river but walking in the grass beside it, and I, being a Bird, just had to join them, so with a few good quacks and Karen on the camera I did so, and got pretty close. "You're just a silly duck yourself," she said.

"Yes, and so are you, sweetheart, making us a good match," I replied.

Hannelori had left us by that time to drive to the end point, Weltenburg. We grabbed a sandwich before loading and paid our two Euros each to board, a real deal for the hour-long cruise. With the sandwich in my tummy and the duck experience in hand, I was feeling much better about the whole boat-ride thing.

"I do have good ideas," Karen said, looking me in the eye. This again was absolutely true. I agreed and kissed her velvety cheek, which I am free to do at almost any time, another marvelous benefit of abandoning bachelorhood.

We marched across the gangplank together and onto the spacious boat with about 50 others, finding an interior table with a view. Delicious apple strudel and tea arrived soon after and then we headed upstairs to the open upper deck, where we watched with great interest while passing between the high rock walls of one of the more scenic portions of the river.

This was the holiday we had hoped for. Our ride ended at a monastery at Weltenburg, where Hannelori and car awaited.

"Did you enjoy it?" she asked.

"We did, and thanks so much for making it happen," I said, grateful once again for the life-enriching quality of family.

Chapter 21

Walter's Little Walk

"YOU REALLY SHOULD rent a car. I can get you a good deal."

Karen had heard this before from her well-intentioned cousin, Walter Langenberger. He and his wife Keirsten operated a travel agency out of their home in Wildsteig, a village in the foothills of the Alps.

No doubt, Walter was trying to help. He couldn't imagine travel without car rental, as he had visited Canada and toured by car. I, on the other hand, had been to Germany before and knew we really didn't need wheels. Given Germany's excellent train and bus systems, I felt we simply wouldn't have any use for a car.

Yet almost every time Karen talked to him prior to our May trip, Walter brought the subject up and had my wife half-convinced.

Finally, I'd heard enough, as it was causing strain. As we sat in Ingolstadt one day, enjoying our time with cousin Hannelori Freitmeier, Karen phoned Walter to let him know our time of arrival by train in a centre near their home. When he pushed the car-rental plan yet again, I talked to him and explained that we honestly didn't want one.

A few days later our train ride south was delightful and inexpensive. Walter -- mid-50ish, of medium height and red hair, a former competitive skier and an avid cyclist -- met us and drove us to his home in Wildsteig, chatting all the while about points of interest.

In Wildsteig he'd booked us into a bed and breakfast at a dairy farm. Our balcony overlooked a pasture. In one corner of the property the family had built their own little church. Sweet.

It was peaceful and just what the doctor ordered, and we were grateful and said so. In the distance the low hills of the Alps sat invitingly. We discovered lovely paths through the forests and fields and even a lake to swim in. These trails provided some lovely walks.

As we visited with Walter and Keirsten, Karen and I told them we'd much rather walk or cycle than drive.

"We walked for days in England, you know," we explained.

Then I told them about my walk and run across Manitoba in winter to raise money for Heart and Stroke. We were active people.

Why not walk a bit in the Alps? But maybe, just maybe, we laid it on too thick. Walter had an idea, he told us cheerily, a favourite trail of his that he'd done a few times. It sounded promising, just the ticket. But it was 12 kilometres one way (7.5 miles) -- 15 miles return. And you drove some distance just to get there.

"Very nice trail with a creek beside it, a forest like in Canada," he assured us.

"It's too long for a day trip," I said. This must have sounded pretty feeble after all our bragging.

"It is not a problem," he insisted. I suspected he'd cycled it rather than walked it, as his knees, he explained later, couldn't take the strain of walking. But I didn't push the matter further. We were the guests, after all, and his heart was in this. The day of the walk, one thing led to another, delaying our start, and by the time we actually got there it was 1:30 p.m. At first it was fine. But the trail kept going and going, higher and higher, in scenery much like that of a Port Alberni logging road: a little bit goes a long way.

It wasn't so much a walking path as a cycling trail and paved road, and Walter rode his bike. Karen, myself and Keirsten were on foot. We met some people but few walkers; most people cycled, and the ones headed down sure had a head of steam. Karen, always a good sport, took it in stride. I began to growl. And after three hours of uphill slogging, my patience and goodwill were like my shoes -- wearing thin. Three hours should have been a round trip.

"You know, Walter," I said, taking him aside, "this is too much for people on a visit. We are office workers, not marathoners, and we are not in great shape."

The girls began to talk about it, too, with Keirsten telling a story of the "friend" whom Walter had invited to cycle this area a few years ago. The man had arrived pleased and excited. But after two days with Walter, strained and exhausted, he left in a huff and never called again.

Meanwhile, our host assured us repeatedly that the top was near. "Just around the corner." Karen and I smiled. His wife laughed.

We plodded on and came to a simple old cabin where fresh water poured into a rustic wooden trough. Open fields spread out before the cabin. My kind of place. It wasn't the end of the trail, though it probably should have been.

Walter urged us on. The girls went. The view ahead, after all, was said to be breathtaking.

I decided to wait at the cabin for their return, enjoying a nap in the grass. This was, after all, our holiday. Finally, being on a bike, Walter sped down the hill and drove his car up to get us. There was no way we'd have made it back on foot in anywhere near time for supper, and we were hungry.

"I guess it was pretty far," Keirsten said as we drove down the mountain. At the bottom, with some laughs about Walter's "little walk," we scarfed down a restaurant meal.

We learned, once again, to be careful what you ask for, because you might just get it.

Chapter 22

Neuschwanstein Castle

MAYBE KING LUDWIG II wasn't so crazy after all. He was the energy behind the construction of many castles, including the famous Neuschwanstein Castle in the Bavarian Alps of Germany. If you've ever seen the Walt Disney Show on TV, you've seen an animated likeness of Neuschwanstein.

Karen and I took a little trip there when we visited Bavaria. Ludwig II is often referred to as the "mad king." He frequently dined alone, but insisted his servants set places for imaginary guests. He also used to paddle around alone in a moat and listen to opera. (Take note, opera buffs.) But look at the facts: Neuschwanstein (literally 'new swan stone', as he loved swans) draws hundreds of thousands of visitors a year, earns millions of dollars for the Bavarian people, and is the biggest tourism draw in the land.

Mad? Maybe, rather, a far-sighted eccentric. He probably liked cats. In any case, Karen and I were taken there by our hosts, Walter and Keirsten Langenberger, who live in the village of Wildsteig, population 1,235, an hour's drive away. Walter is a second cousin to Karen, someone she last saw 30 years ago. He and his wife are travel agents and have their own business.

Walter was sure we'd enjoy the trip and we did. Upon our arrival we were amazed by all the people and had a quick bite to eat before the long walk to the actual castle, which is perched on a hillside. There we joined the cattle lines through its massive shell for a peek at what German royalty thought fine in the 1860s.

The view from the castle is stunning, a panoramic spectacle of orderly farms, picturesque villages and a large lake. Construction began in 1869, pretty late in the day for castle construction if you know your medieval history, and the peasants at the time weren't pleased. The crazy king was squandering their hard-earned shekels on what they considered an inane white elephant.

The king was murdered (possibly drowned, but there was no water in his lungs) in 1886 before he fully settled into his new home

-- a cautionary tale indeed for politicians pondering large projects. But Ludwig would have liked the castle, as it was equipped with all kinds of technical conveniences which were very modern, if not revolutionary at the time, including water on all floors. The spring which supplied the castle with drinking water was only 200 meters above it. There were toilets equipped with automatic flushing on every floor, a warm air heating system for the entire building, a hot water system for the kitchen and the bath – better, in some ways, than homes in 20th-century England and Canada.

The Throne Room (not, perhaps, what first leaps to mind) was designed in elaborate Byzantine style and was inspired by the Hagia Sophia in Constantinople (now Istanbul). Today, the throne is missing. The royal bedroom features incredible woodcarvings. Fourteen carvers are said to have worked 4 1/2 years on the room. "The Monarch's bed is crowned by the most intricate woodcarving and covered with richly embroidered draperies," a site explains.

We shuffled through the room with hundreds of others, truly enthralled by the extravagance of it all. Even today there's a fine line between beauty, such as a fancy new house, and gaudiness. This appeared to lean towards the latter.

Back at Wildsteig, we explored the lovely little village and found it enchanting, with a great little bakery and a pond with fish in the central "square." Nearby are lots of trails for walking and biking in the easy foothills of the Alps. We much preferred the village to the castle.

Karen and I spent many happy hours wandering those pathways through forests and flower-filled pastures. Dairy cows wore bells that jangled in the sun. The fields were alive with many colourful flowers, since chemicals are banned in farming there.

We loved the sweet smell of the air and the beauty of the landscape. We'd go back to Wildsteig any time, as our second-storey suite on a dairy farm was a honeymooner's love nest, and it cost only 25 Euros ($40) a night -- and that included four fresh eggs and milk each morning.

Thanks to Walter we were also treated to an evening of local song and dance at the community hall. Everyone was decked out in their Bavarian costumes. A mother-daughter yodeling duo stole the show, which featured a super Swiss chorus as well.

The castle was okay, but Karen and I preferred the simpler attractions like good food, good walks, traditional music and jangling cow bells.

Chapter 23

Mittenwald

A TRAIN RIDE APPEALED to us, and so we left Wildsteig one day and headed for Mittenwald, near Austria. We disembarked and found ourselves face to face with a mountain so close you could touch it. Mittenwald's grandiose setting is at the junction of the Wetterstein and Karwendel ranges.

You know the Bugs Bunny cartoon where Yosemite Sam keeps sliding down a mountain into a town to the sound of a brass band? I thought of this as we gazed at the wall of granite behind us. We were 3,000 feet up in the Alps on Germany's extreme southern border, spitting distance from Austria.

Mittenwald (which means "middle forest") is a market town of 7,900 people. It's a pretty village setting and easy to get around on foot. It started to rain as my wife and I walked into the nearby business district, and while Karen went off to check out some souvenir shops I found a cafe with umbrellas up to keep its patrons dry. This was June, mid-afternoon.

I found a good chair and relaxed, sat back and watched the world go by. To my back was the cafe and mountain, while the view before me was of a busy street of shops and plenty of pedestrians. No cars.

It wasn't long before a lone traveler sat down at a table in front of mine. He was a fair-haired young fellow who appeared to be in his early 20s. His clothes were worn, like my own, and he was thin, so he wasn't likely affluent. He wore a bandanna around his forehead and a blue windbreaker.

After a few minutes he ordered a plate of fish. It looked delicious and I said as much. He looked at me, agreed, and proceeded to polish it off.

"I'll have the same, please," I told the waiter as he took my order.

"Have you been traveling long?" I asked the young man.

"I have a one-month ticket to anywhere in Europe," he said. It had cost him 600 Euros, about $900 Cdn. And he had three weeks to gad about, with the first week just up.

His name was Antti Poso, he said, and he was a mailman from Helsinki, Finland. He said he enjoyed delivering letters, as the exercise made him feel good. I was a little off in my estimate of his age; Antti told me he was 28. He'd just finished a master's degree in history, "but it's hard to find a job in your area."

I told him people in Canada were having a similar problem, and then asked how the recession had affected his country. "People talk about it a lot," he said, "and of course there is cutting of labour. But it's not as bad as it was when we had a recession in the early 1990s."

I told him Finnish people had a reputation for being happy. "I think the Danish are the most happy in the whole world," he replied. I asked him why that was, but he wasn't sure.

He'd worked the previous summer in Denmark for six weeks at a fish processing plant. "At first there were no fish and no work," he said. "We had to wait over a week," for which he wasn't paid.

Antti told me he was looking forward to meeting up with his girlfriend in Barcelona in a few days. "But I need the experience of traveling on my own, first."

I told him that was a good plan; traveling with a woman is a wonderful thing but different from being alone. I said I enjoyed travel both ways, and hoped he would find the flexibility to do the same.

He smiled knowingly.

"So tell me about your work," I said. He does the 7 to 3 shift, and said he doesn't walk too far, "it's mostly big buildings, with many stairs."

Both of his parents were teachers. His mother lived 50 kilometers east of Helsinki, he said. His father had died young at 54 from a heart attack. "It was a very devastating time for our family," he said. Antti was 22 when it happened.

Just then Karen approached, smiling and wet but obviously pleased to find me where I'd said I'd be.

"Karen, this is Antti Poso; Antti, my wife Karen. He and I have been having a chat. Antti was just telling me how his father died about the same age your father passed on, and how hard it was."

Karen picked up on that and asked him about it. The rain began to fall heavier and after a few minutes we decided to move into the cafe proper, where it was also a lot warmer.

My meal arrived, and Karen ordered, and we treated Antti to a beer. He told us he had a dog, which he adored, at his mother's place, and it was the same breed the Obamas have at the White House.

He knew a little German but found it hard to understand what people said, so he resorted to English, mostly. Karen said she did much the same.

After a bit we rose to leave, and wished him the best. I felt energized and happy. I guess you can take the reporter out of the office, but you can't take the curiosity out of the reporter, no matter where he or she is.

And sometimes – often, in fact – people enjoy sharing their story. Antti, I think, was sorry to see us leave.

Chapter 24

The Isle of Wight – Again

AFTER OUR VISIT to Mittenwald, Karen and I met her family at the nearby town of Oberau, and had supper together at the Maximilian Hotel, one of the fanciest joints there. Good thing the rellies were paying!

Chef Alexander Schutz, a large man (good to see in a cook) came to our table and told us he learned his craft in France, where both food prep and consumption take much longer than in Germany.

His Kaiserschmarrn (pancake with apples flambé) was delicious, as was the maxbrau beer, brewed on site. But our time in Germany was up, and I was eager to take Karen to England's Isle of Wight, which I had enjoyed the year before but she hadn't seen, having gone home for business. This was early June, 2009.

At Lymington on England's south coast we boarded the ferry for Yarmouth, and 20 minutes later were there. I felt at home. I just love the Isle of Wight: its smallness, quaintness, lack of fast traffic, proximity to the ocean, beautiful old buildings and awesome green spaces, including walking trails through idyllic farm country with sheep and horses never far away.

We strolled around little old Yarmouth for a while and after knocking on a few doors found a room at the Jirah Guest House and dumped our bags. It was late afternoon but we still had lots of daylight left, and we only had this day and the next on the Isle.

We crossed the bridge over the River Yar and headed south along a pathway towards a place I'd visited the first time, Freshwater. It was so lush and warm and delightful that I can never understand why more people don't visit the Isle. Even my own English relatives and friends turn their noses up when I wax enthusiastically about Wight. It's a puzzle.

At least Karen liked it. At one point she wanted to head back to Yarmouth, feeling hungry, but we kept going, thankfully. I say thankfully because soon after that we saw little furry animals, likely bunnies, across one of the fields. Then, not 20 minutes later, we came to The Red Lion, a pub where I'd met the Viking man and his Gypsy wife, whom I wrote about last year. We feasted, ordering whatever we liked, including fish and lamb. The food and beer were delicious.

"Whaddya know, buddy?" I said to a guy in his early 60s, lean and friendly-looking, sitting at the bar. "Now this is a meal," I said.

"The food's good here," said Joe, a semi-retired carpenter. He came over and sat at our table and we chewed the fat for a long time. I didn't take notes -- too busy talking and eating – but we enjoyed Joe's company.

"This is wonderful, Brad," Karen said.

"Now you know why I wanted to bring you here," I said.

The walk back to Jirah House was even more enchanting in the twilight. Near the Red Lion there's a plaque on a fence with a story about a drunken sailor who was the butt of a practical joke. He'd got liquored up pretty badly sometime in the 1800s and his mates plunked him down at Freshwater, telling him it was the French coast. He wandered around, asking people about this and that, as if he were in France, and the locals thought he was loony.

Next day, after breakfast, we took a bus to Totland and walked toward the Needles, which are chalk rocks jutting out of the sea. It was a beautiful day and soon we were walking on a hillside called Headon Warren.

It was great up there, sunny and with a super view of the water. At one point we found an old foundation site that maybe the Romans had built during their time there. We came upon a par-3 golf course. "Let's have a game," I said, and Karen agreed. It was fun knocking the balls around and we really enjoyed it. The lady who ran the place was helpful -- especially when we told her we'd lost our camera. I figured we'd left it at the old site on the Warren and started back, when Karen and the woman located it at one of our holes.

We met a nice bunch of people at a picnic table there and chatted awhile, then headed on towards the Needles.

We got a bite to eat at Needles Park, took some photos and headed back to Yarmouth. That afternoon we left Wight for Poole and visited Ted Larkins, one of Dad's air force crewmen from 1944. Ted was well and we had a good visit. Cousin Dorothy Pollard was next on the list at Hillside near Oxford.

Then, reluctantly, we flew home, our visits to Germany and England at an end. Until next time.

Chapter 25

'Where Are You Going Now?'

IT WAS SEPTEMBER of 2005, and I had itchy feet. Again.

Five months earlier, I'd walked and run 1,000 miles, about 1,600 kilometres, to Churchill on my Border to the Bay trip for Heart and Stroke research. That journey had taken three months. What I planned in September would be much shorter.

A few words about Border to the Bay, which one day should be a book in itself. To get to Churchill I left home on Jan. 25 and arrived some 90 or so days later, on April 15, after sleeping mostly outside in the snow. There'd been a few storms and some -30 degree C cold. One morning my thermometer registered -40. But I made it, thanks to good equipment (including a Mountain Equipment Co-op sleeping bag rated at -30 C and a sled which carried my gear). The journey raised about $14,000 for the Heart and Stroke Foundation, and I thoroughly enjoyed the trip. I could see how the Metis and native peoples of old could travel that way. I had a lot of help from people along the way, and will always be grateful to them for the warm beds and hot food they provided.

As fall came on, I felt an urge to walk again. I missed the fun and adventure. I missed the feeling of well-being, both mental and physical. I missed the sense of purpose. I'm not very good at being happy when living in a house; I find it too sedentary and boring, the same walls each day, not enough change or purpose. I like to be on the move. Heck, I almost *need* to be moving, chasing a goal.

When I traveled as a newspaperman abroad, the goal was stories. Get here to do that interview; go there to get that story. That had been the pattern in North Africa, Kosovo and Turkey, in Greece and Hungary and Germany. I liked the constant change, the new faces, foods and places the traveling life dished up. Often I was away for months at a time.

Now I was eager to hit the road again. On August 28, Hurricane Katrina hit the southern coast of the United States with devastating effect, as you'll remember. It was reported that more than 1,800 people lost their lives, and some $81 billion in damage was done. They needed help of all kinds. Here was another cause worth walking for.

When the storm hit, I was living at my home in southwest Manitoba at Lake Metigoshe on Turtle Mountain on the Manitoba-North Dakota border. That was home for 11 years. I should say a bit about the mountain, because it wasn't a true mountain, being only 600 to 800 feet above the surrounding plains. Some 25 miles across north-south and east-west, Turtle Mountain was shaped like a turtle, a large patch of forest, lakes and wetlands, home to countless beaver, muskrats and mink; moose, white-tailed deer and some elk; great horned owls, golden eagles and vultures; pelicans, red-headed grebes and loons. Oh, the loons and their mystical calls – when they sang in flight, you knew that rain was coming. Where they swam, you knew there were fish. In many of the shallow lakes were northern pike, walleye and perch, with some trout as well. Turtle Mountain, a remnant, in part, of the last glaciation 10 millennium ago, was a year-round vacationer's dream, and for local farmers and townspeople in and around Boissevain, Deloraine, Melita and Waskada, it was the place to be.

Home for me was a 66-foot trailer I'd bought in The Pas. That was a great place to live, too, but that's another story. See *Me and My Canoe* if you like. I only had a postage stamp-sized lot at Metigoshe, but it was mine. It was close to the water and farmland and forests where I hunted and trapped. It was also close to the U.S. border, which in fact was my southern property line. I was as close to Florida as a guy could get in Manitoba. The trailer faced south, so it was bathed in sun year round. This always cheered me.

I loved the four seasons, the changes and challenges that went with each on the mountain. Spring was my favourite, with its newness, fresh growth, returning geese, renewed hope for the heat and fun of summer. Spring, with its trapping, receding snows, longer days, warm weather, was a respite from the bone-chilling cold. Summer offered endless sunny days, saskatoons and raspberries plump and tasty, cooling swims and exciting fishing for pike and walleye. Summer provided farm work, endless sunshine, booming thunderstorms and quiet canoeing.

Fall, my least favourite, the death season, was a prelude to winter's wonderland, a start to trapping when the muskrats and beavers primed up, but it always tended to leave me melancholy. Winter, like summer a pure season, not a transition state, restored my cheerfulness with ice fishing, trapping, moon-lit walks, snowmobiling, cross-country skiing, curling -- and Hockey Night in Canada on the TV by my wood stove, with Jimmy by my side, purring.

I enjoyed being alone, independent and free. But I wasn't totally alone. Three cats were my principal companions: Jimmy, Buddy and Kali. Jimmy was the eldest and had come first. I'd taken him in, I think in December of 1995, after the people across the street left to seek work in Brandon. It was a cold winter day and I was out cutting firewood and talking to a neighbour when we heard this yowling. "That's a cat," said Dave Wall. We headed over to the vacant house and up through the floorboards of the covered porch emerged a very thin and very cold kitten, black and white. He soon lived with me, and what a great cat he turned out to be. Polite good company was Jimmy. Then a few years later Dave and I were having coffee with Brian Jasper one morning when I noticed he had about six kittens scurrying about. He wanted rid of them. One, with four white socks and a white nose and gray overall, climbed up my pant leg into my lap. She looked at me with the cutest face and nicest eyes. This was Buddy. "Well, look at you," I said, petting the soft creature. We bonded.

"That's one gone," said Dave, eyeing the situation. I took Buddy home and found she needed a playmate, so next day I relieved Brian of another kitten, a calico he'd named Kali. That's how I got my three cats.

At first Jimmy resented the new arrivals. He acted like an old man suddenly faced with an influx of bothersome grandchildren. Or an uncle dealing with meddlesome nephews. I settled on the uncle metaphor and called him Uncle Jimmy. But the kittens they won him over. They spent time with Uncle Jimmy and showed him respect, usually, or they got a swat. I knew all would be OK one day when I watched Jimmy bring home a field mouse dangling from his teeth, which he then set down in front of Buddy, who proceeded to throw it about and play with it before eating it. I'm sure old Jim did the same for Kali. Before long they were good mousers themselves.

And I had good friends in the area: Ernie Goodon, Sue and Larry Black, Lawrence and Ella Canada, David Neufeld and his wife, Ben and Gerrie Kroeker, Don Dietrich and others. Among the best were Dave and Madeleine Wall, who lived across the street. I learned a lot from Dave, about trapping and building and life in general. Dave was a retired carpenter and house builder and electronics man in his 70s, and one of the most amazing guys I know. He was a true Renaissance man who could talk about almost any field of endeavor, but he was superbly practical and good with his hands. Thanks to Dave I had water in my trailer. Thanks to him I had shelter when I first arrived in December 1994, as he led the way as we patched up the old trailer on site at the time. A former TV repairman, he could build anything, fix anything. He built his own home as well as many others in the district. He shingled his own roof. He was a good trapper and hunter (both bow and rifle) and a superb gardener. He and Madeleine put away many jars of pickles, beets and other preserves each year. In the hard early years they'd canned deer meat.

I turned to Dave when I needed a cart to carry a tent, sleeping bags, clothes and food. Within days he had fashioned a two-wheeled cart using all scrounged materials from the nearby dump. Two old bicycle wheels, copper tubing for a frame (which he soldered), and a platform made from the door of an old fridge, plus a handle. The man's a genius.

The trip I envisioned would take about 10 days and see me trek across Turtle Mountain to the east side, south on Highway 21 into North Dakota and round and about there until heading back up Highway 10 toward Boissevain and home across the mountain again.

On Monday, Sept. 26 I left home, after phoning Paul Rayner of Boissevain to tell him. Paul was a friend but also the Boissevain Recorder's award-winning reporter.

"I'm going for another walk. A short one this time."

"Where are you going now?"

"North Dakota, near Rugby. I'd like to raise some money for Red Cross Hurricane relief. They've been hit pretty hard along the Gulf."

"Do you have a target figure?"

"No, I'll get whatever I get. It'll be more than they had."

"When do you leave?"

"Right now, after I finish talking to you. We'll have a beer when I get back."

"You don't have to go for a walk to have the beer, Brad."
"I know. But I like to walk."

So began my 150-mile or 260-km walk for Hurricane Relief. Man, if felt good to hit the pavement again. It was a sunny and warm day when I left home and the prospect was for continued good weather.

Paul's father, by the way, is Vic Rayner, who is quite a fisherman. He's caught lots of Master Angler fish, including rainbow trout, walleye and pike. Vic was a good friend of my late grandfather, Dr. Fred Bird. They fished and hunted together, and when Vic was a boy my grandfather patched him up during and after hockey games. Vic was a tough player and grandpa admired that in a guy. I liked his cheerfulness. He always had a smile and a positive outlook when I visited the Rayner home, where Paul had a suite in the basement.

With the buggy rolling alongside, I walked from home north, toward Canada Corner where Bill and Esther Canada lived. I stopped in for tea with this nice couple, as I had earlier on my trek to Churchill.

The landscape featured the big sky of the Prairie, hay and wheat fields, and a forest of mainly aspen, birch, ash, bur oak and willow. The mountain offered a rolling landscape and forest rare on the flatter lands below. The mountain also cradled many lakes, which made it a prime holiday destination for farmers and townspeople. I felt like I was part of the dirt there, since my father, uncle and grandfather had traipsed that land and hunted that bush and fished those waters since 1913, when Dr. Bird first arrived. He lived in Boissevain for about 62 years until his death in 1977, just short of his 92nd birthday.

I turned west on a gravel road and got to the four corners at 5 p.m. It took me 50 minutes to chug up the hill to Maggie and Owen's place, where I'd been invited to dinner. I looked back at one point and saw a boy on a bike approaching.

"Hi," he said, looking at my buggy. "Where you going?"

"To Rugby," I said.

"What for?

"To raise money for the Red Cross. Hurricane relief. I'm Brad Bird."

"I know who you are. You spoke at our school (about the Border to the Bay walk)."

"What's your name?" I asked.

"Brady Caswell. I live back there. This is some hill, isn't it? My grandpa lives up here, and I can't pedal there it's so tough. Have to get off and walk."

"It is steep. I'm heading for Owen Jones's place. Know it?"

"It's just ahead. Up this hill, down a bit, up again. It gets worse." And he turns around.

"See you," I say.

"I'll be back."

And he was, a few minutes later. "You were right," I said. "This hill does get worse. I'm tempted to leave my buggy here. Maybe not. How old are you, anyway?

"Almost 10." And he chatted some more about his grandfather, as I sweated. Finally I pulled into Owen and Margaret's place, where the boy was right at home, teasing Margaret, who returned the favour.

"You'd best get yourself home, Brady. Your dad'll be lookin' for you."

"I will." He teased the two again and then left.

Around me was a veritable museum of old boat motors, chain saws, lumber, and any number of unidentifiable items lost in the tall grass. A large garden, harvested but for some rows of cucumbers, sat idle one side of the lane. The house was comfortable and well aged, and sat beyond an old pickup full of tools. This was the Jones's home.

"We don't get many visitors," Maggie said.

"You can set up your tent anywhere you like," Owen said, and we discussed the options.

Inside, roasted moose meat was served up with potatoes, macaroni, pickles and fresh white buns. Delicious, I said. Owen shared with me some of his coveted finds at local refuse pits: chinaware, the chairs we sit on, the boat motors, Christmas ornaments, you name it, he's recycled and made good use of it. And they take real satisfaction in saving this stuff from the ignominy of being buried forever.

I shared some of my finds: shoes, gloves, records, a Queen Elizabeth teacup and saucer, an old canoe I repaired. We ate some more.

They had two dogs, a big one and a little one. A cat lived mostly in the cellar to control the mice.

After more conversation outside, I got into my tent and slept.

Chapter 26

'It's a Sex Number'

Day TWO, SEPT. 27, began with a good breakfast cooked by Maggie, and then I headed out. She and Owen offered to pick me up about 11 a.m. near Joan and Maurice Lesy's place and take me into Deloraine for a dental appointment. Teeth cleaning time. This worked out great, and I asked them if they'd mind running me back to my trailer for stuff I wanted to pick up.

First, though, I treated them to lunch at Bee Jay's restaurant, the least I could do for all their help. We phoned to confirm the arrival of my new laptop in Boissevain but decided to go to my place first. The laptop would accompany me on the trip and allow me to write regular updates.

By the time I got back to my buggy it was 4:30 and chances are I wouldn't see Dunc Stewart that night. I'd arranged to possibly meet him near Highway 21. I got to within a mile and a half of 21 and camped for the night in an oak bluff. Dunc and I and Maurice Lesy had sung with the Southwest Singers, and we car pooled.

When I awoke next morning at 7:15 in my wooded campsite, the thermometer registered 2C. The small forest of bur oaks provided shelter from the blustery north wind that settled in the previous afternoon. I slept well in my down-filled sleeping bag in this protected site, which is a horse pasture ringed with barbed wire. I heard the horse in the night but he didn't hang around to chat.

It was Sept. 28, 2005, Day 3 of a walk from my home on Turtle Mountain into North Dakota to raise money for Hurricane relief.

As I headed west toward Highway 21, the view was beautiful. I'd slept in the last of the wooded areas, but the golden hay fields, big round bales and distant wood lots were beautiful to behold. The walking was easy too, as the downhill slope encouraged my buggy along to the point where I had to hold back a bit, like a wagon driver holding back his team. Except I was the team.

I warmed up quickly despite the chill in the air and soon was on Highway 21 and heading south. Very few vehicles on the road which was good. This early in the trip I felt self-conscious about pulling a buggy and being conspicuous on the highway.

Stopping for breakfast near a ravine, I suddenly heard a squalling or shrieking sound from the forest. I put it down to porcupines mating; they make quite a fuss (no wonder, with all those quills involved). The cold oatmeal and apples went down well. But just as I was putting away my bowl, I looked up to see a full-grown raccoon trucking north on the southbound lane only a few metres away.

"Hey, what's up?" I shouted. The animal ignored me and kept trotting north. I followed, with camera in hand, and seemed to be gaining on it. Ever tried to take a photo while running? I was about to click the shutter when he pulled hard left into the high grass of the ravine. Even then I followed him, hoping for another chance, but the grass was in the way. Maybe the wailing I'd heard was a couple of coons in dispute.

Down at the Goodlands port, I stopped in at the Canadian Customs Office. Customs Officer Noreen Nestibo was working at a computer as I entered the office. We chatted a bit, and she told me she remembered me from the time I'd been to her family's greenhouse to write a story for the *Deloraine Times & Star* some years ago. With her permission I plugged in the laptop to charge it up, and also shaved.

Noreen seemed to like the idea of raising money for Hurricane relief, and wished me well. Another lady who was cleaning took a moment of her time to snap a photo of me and the rig.

"I'm off to U.S. Customs," I told them. "Thanks."

"Have a good trip and good luck with our friends there," Noreen said, hinting that it might not be easy. She was right!

At 10:45 a.m. I arrived at the U.S. Port. I walked in and met the Port Director, Mr. Scott Ceglowski, and a Mr. Williamson. They gave me a friendly greeting and asked me to pull the buggy off to the side. They were interested in the purpose of my trip and were polite throughout. Still, it was an interesting three hours. It took that long to be cleared to go.

"Please empty your pockets."

I did so, including a small knife that was held by the boss for the duration. Meanwhile, Mr. Williamson went through my gear outside. The standard questions were asked -- how long I'd be down for, where I'd be going.

"Will you be leaving anything in North Dakota?"

"No." Afterwards I thought, yes -- a little goodwill.

This visit was different because of the fund-raising venture for the American Red Cross in Minot. I was asked for a letter from them, but didn't have one.

"You could phone them and talk to the executive director," I said. "He'll confirm what I've told you."

Mr. Ceglowski liked this idea and took the 1 800 number I offered and went to phone. Then we waited. And waited.

Meanwhile, Mr. Williamson returned from his search of my gear with two cans of Chef Boyardee Mini Bites, a type of ravioli. "I'm sorry, but we have to take these," he said. "There's beef in them. I know the ban has been lifted (on Canadian beef exports to the U.S. owing to Mad Cow disease) but we have our rules to follow. Sorry."

"That's OK," I said. "Would it be OK if I ate the contents of one of the cans while I waited?"

"Sure."

Better eaten than wasted. Besides, I was hungry. It was 11:30 now and I was ready for lunch.

Mr. Ceglowski came out from his office at 12:10. He didn't look pleased.

"That number you gave me isn't the Red Cross. It's a sex number."

"A sex number?" I said, surprised, but also ready to laugh.

"Yes, "he said, stern-faced. "I called it twice."

"Golly, there must have been some mistake," I said. "Look, is it OK if I go to my gear and get my original notes? Maybe I took it down wrong."

Go ahead, he said.

I returned with the pad and read off the number: 1 800 323-3179--"

"There's the problem," he said. "You had 3279 here."

"Gee, I'm so sorry," I said. "I was rushed when I wrote it."

"No problem. We'll try again." And he went to phone.

More waiting.

Williamson was busy so I looked around a bit. Ahead of me was a long counter. On each side was an office, with the boss's to my right. It had a window in the door but I couldn't see him at his desk. On the left wall was a Manitoba Highways map. Straight ahead were photos of President Bush, and the head of internal security, and some other chap, in that order. I thought Bush would have been in the centre but he wasn't.

Below them was a cork board with an image of Uncle Sam. He was urging people to help stop drug smuggling. Along the back of the building appeared to be a coffee room.

A cheerful man whom I took to be a border patrol guy entered and we chatted a fair bit about my journey and different things. "It's time's like this a man's glad to have lived a clean life," I said to him. "I don't go in for stupidities such as drugs, crime, etc. -- things that prevent a guy from traveling."

He agreed. "Yeah, that stuff is just plain stupid." After a while he left.

I had received permission by this time to bring in my laptop and plug it in to charge the battery. I'd just purchased it the day before in Boissevain and intended to keep my journal on it directly, instead of writing in longhand. It would save a step and inspire me to maybe keep it up to date better. I was content sitting there, knowing that when I left, I'd do so with a fully charged computer that was good for three hours without hydro.

Mr. Williamson returned from his office to my left and seemed willing to chat.

"Do you like hockey?" I asked him.

"No. I hate hockey. My kids play, and some parents, they think it's a salvation or something. Bottineau parents had a meeting and talked about joining the Manitoba league -- Deloraine, Boissevain and that, nice and close. But somebody said, "Well, they're pretty rough up there." So it was decided to play in the North Dakota league. But our games are in Montana and Grand Forks and such places, a long way from here."

"That must cost a fortune in gas," I said.

"It does. And on top of that the games are usually Friday or Saturday, so we have to stay in these places overnight."

"And pay hotel and restaurant bills."

"Yes."

I told him how I'd played a year of organized hockey as a kid in Toronto, but found it unpleasant, with parents shouting and kids crying because they feared what their dads would say when they flubbed a scoring chance.

"Yes, I have a boy who's mild mannered. Strangely enough, he likes the game more than the other boy."

Mr. Ceglowski came out and picked up my passport off the counter, then returned to his office.

"We're getting closer," the hockey parent said.

"So where did you come from originally?" I asked.

"Ohio. My wife's from North Dakota, and we were up in Alaska for a while. I've been here two years -- and you're the first guy I've seen walk through this port."

I went out to my buggy (this time without asking) and pumped some air into my tires. Then I plucked a shirt that needed sewing out of my gear. Inside again, I sewed the ripped sleeve. And jotted some notes. Be patient, Brad, I kept telling myself. These men have a job to do. This is post-9/11. Security is tight, and you're a bit eccentric.

The signed letter arrived from the Red Cross in Minot -- but I wasn't off the hook yet. Mr. Ceglowski had more questions.

"You were in Istanbul recently. Why?"

"To do academic research for my Master's thesis. I graduated in June with an MA in Political Studies from the University of Manitoba."

"Who did you see in Turkey?"

He might not like it if I told him people sympathetic to the PKK, a rebel group, so I didn't. "Academics, mainly," I said. "Professors at Bilkent University, including two American fellows who were of great help."

He asked for the spelling of Bilkent and I provided it. "Did you visit any other countries?"

"Just England. Again, to do research for the thesis."

"What was the thesis about?"

"It was about the war between the Turkish state and the PKK, which is a Kurdish militant group. You see, they'd been fighting for 15 years, a bloody war with 30,000 dead, and then suddenly in 1999 peace broke out. Or seemed to. The title is "Explaining Peace: Turkey and the Kurdish Insurrection." I wanted to find out why peace, or at least a long cease-fire, had broken out at that particular time. You see," I said, warming to my topic, "if we could learn what caused peace then, we might be able to apply that knowledge to other conflicts such as the Israeli-Palestinian dispute, or the fighting in Sri Lanka."

"What did you find out?

"Well, I applied three theories. First, realism. That's basically power politics. What had happened is that the Turks, with American and Israeli assistance, had captured the leader of the PKK in early 1999. His name is Abdullah Ocalan. With him in jail, that essentially beheaded the PKK and left it weak. Shortly afterwards he declared a ceasefire while in custody. He's in prison now. So it seemed that power politics worked.

"The second theory I applied was democratic peace theory. This basically holds that democratic reforms such as increased rights of expression serve to reduce grievances. Turkey indeed was giving the Kurds greater freedoms -- they could speak Kurdish freely and even broadcast in it, for example -- and this clearly, in my view, contributed to the ceasefire. But I stressed that it remained brittle peace, one that could easily be broken.

"Thirdly I applied economic development theory. This holds that as you provide people with jobs and income and stability, again their grievances are reduced -- that is their motivation to rebel is reduced. They are building big dams in the southeast of Turkey that on the face of it are supposed to help fuel development. But in fact they aren't, because most of the power is shipped west to the industrial west of Turkey. The Kurdish southeast has no factories, you see. So this theory didn't apply."

"And you concluded what."

"I concluded that structural realism played a role in the ceasefire -- that is, the capture of Ocalan as a result of the end of bipolar politics. That democratic peace theory had a role to play. And that the other theory didn't. But I stressed that the peace would be brittle because it seemed inevitable to me that other PKK leaders would emerge and urge a resumption of fighting, for whatever reason. They're into the drug trade and have that and status to lose by going clean. And that is exactly what has happened. The fighting resumed, off and on, about 16 months ago."

"Interesting. We're having the same problem with our war on terror," Mr. Williamson pointed out. "We get some of their leaders and other new ones pop up."

"Exactly. It's a tough kind of war to win."

"How long were you in Turkey?"

"About three weeks."

They seemed satisfied, but I waited another hour. Mr. Ceglowski came out of his office. "You see, the other problem is that you will be soliciting for an organization to which you do not belong. I respect your purpose, it's a good cause, but we have had to phone a number of agencies to satisfy them."

"Homeland Security?" I asked.

"A number of agencies. But we can now let you go."

I thanked them very much for their courtesy.

As I walked out the door to my car, Williamson said to me, sotto voice: "You'd better get out of here before they change their mind."

I did.

Chapter 27

Into North Dakota

IT WAS 1:45 and a beautiful afternoon. I left the office feeling great, and began to run. By a quarter to five I'd made quite a few miles. As a Border Patrol truck pulled up, I stopped. At the wheel was a young man in uniform, the same cheerful guy I'd chatted with earlier at the border office. "They let you in, did they?" he asked, with a southern twang and a smile.

"Yes. No problem, really."

"Did they give you an A45 stamp?"

"Yeah," I said. "I have it here with my passport."

"Good. You be sure to show it to Highway Patrol in case they stop you. OK?"

"I will. Thanks." He pulled away and did a U-turn to head north again. I stopped him as he came around. "Would you by chance have any garbage bags? I'm picking up trash as I walk along and mine is full."

"No, I don't. I'd give you an apple or something if I had one." He was chewing on an apple. He popped up the lid on a cooler. "Here, want a bag of Frito's?"

"Sure. Thanks."

"No problem. Stay safe."

"You mean safe on the highway?"

"I mean safe from the cold. It's going down to about 35 tonight."

"I have good gear. I'll be fine."

"OK, have a good trip." And he was gone.

Not long afterwards another visitor stopped to chat. Bottineau Sheriff Steve Watson pulled up in his cruiser. We talked, and he offered a tomato and two cucumbers, and suggested I camp the night at a recreation area a few miles south. He even offered a ride but I declined, not wanting to break the continuity of the trip. It's unsettling to do that, to break up a walk with vehicular help. Very nice man again, though.

Oh, and Sheriff Watson gave me my first donation -- $10. "Good luck on your cause," and he drove off.

I camped about a mile up the road in a ravine by 6 p.m. In bed by 7 and it was a good day all in all.

On Day 4, Thursday Sept. 29, I was up by 7:15 and on the road by 8. Cool, but not as cold as expected. It was 44F or so, about 6 degrees C.

The first few hours were taken up by steady walking. Ideal conditions. A number of cars went by but nobody stopped, for which I was rather thankful. I'd seen enough uniforms for a while.

By 11 a.m. I arrived at Sunny 101.9 Radio station in Bottineau. Outside the station I dumped a green garbage bag full of beer cans, pop cans, cigarette packages and whatnot into their large trash container, and then met one of their sales people at the door. He showed me in and there stood three people: DJ Dylan Connor, manager Rick Gustafson and receptionist Lisa Simonson.

"Hi," I said. "I think I have a story for you."

"What's up?" Dylan said.

"I'm walking to raise money for Red Cross Hurricane Relief."

"Where'd you start?"

"At my home, on the north shore of Metigoshe. I'm Canadian. I'll do a big loop over to Dunseith, down to Rugby, over to Rolla, north to St. John and through the Peace Garden Port and back home."

"How much do you hope to raise?"

"$1000 would be nice. In fact your Sheriff Watson gave me the first $10 yesterday, so all we need are another 99 people to pony up the same amount and we've got $1000 bucks for the Hurricane victims."

"Right on. Sure, we'll do an interview, eh Rick?" He nodded. "Come right into the studio and we'll give you three minutes. We're tight for time with news coming up. Is that OK?"

"Fantastic," I said.

When the song ended -- "she finds my tractor sexy" -- we did my first live interview of the trip. It went well. DJ Dylan Connor was good with the questions and we did a nice three-minute spot.

Receptionist Lisa Simonson and manager Rick Gustafson kicked in $20 for the cause.

Down the road a bit at the bowling alley I phoned the Bottineau Courant and let them know what was happening, then sat down to a nice hot beef sandwich. I'd eaten oatmeal and salmon for breakfast and found a Reese's peanut butter cup on the road (still wrapped), so wasn't too hungry.

Scott Wagar of the Courant arrived as I was writing my journal and we did an interview, and then he took some photos of me on the road. I've talked to Scott before, when I was with the Peace Garden as its program director (providing shows and guided walks for campers). We caught up on news about people we know and had a good chat. It's been a good day, I'm thinking.

A fellow in a while van pulls up and hands me $10. "I've seen you three times now. Here's some money." I've got $40 now on the trip and things are rolling along.

Heading east out of Bottineau, I paused for a while at a cemetery and in the shade pulled out my laptop and wrote my journal. It was too hot to walk. From 1 to 3 I cooled off in the shade.

Back on the pavement, it felt good to know I was keeping on top of my writing. Writing at mid-day also gave my feet a break.

A native man with his wife and child pulled up in a truck and asked if I was taking donations. "Sure am," I tell him. He handed me $10. "You've just done your part. Thanks." And he was gone.

Around 5:30 I was looking for a campsite. There was a woodlot to my left about a kilometer away. A native fellow stopped and chatted and suggested straight ahead a mile. I thanked him but stuck to my plan. I didn't have a mile left in me. I found a fence-line and tree 300 metres off Highway 5, half way to the woodlot, and camped there. A lovely spot. I slept well again.

Some days are busy, like yesterday. Some days are slow, like today, Friday, Day 5. Walking and more walking. Self talk and more self talk. Keep it up, get to Dunseith. Think of the restaurant there. Dale's, I think it's called. Clean up, wash hair, shave, do the shirts in a sink. Just keep going, I tell myself.

But it was so hot, 25 C or more, 80 or more F. Nobody stopped to talk or donate. At a culvert, some water, cool water in a tractor track soothed the feet. Blisters on my right foot. Damn. Popped one yesterday, wet and oozing.

Finally, I get to Dunseith. Started walking at 7:45 a.m. and it's 12:45 when I arrive, almost out of water. Roast beef dinner first. Delicious. That's one thing about walking. Food tastes so much better when you've really earned it. Sleep is better too.

I write and write some more in the cool comfort of the dining room, a Coke and hot meal at my fingertips. Few people around me -- it's after 1.

"Would you like to donate to Red Cross Hurricane relief?" I asked young waitress having a smoke break behind the building where I parked my buggy.

"Have no cash on me, just my tips. And I have to hand them in. I bought $5 worth of chocolate bars from my sister yesterday. They're raising money for it too, in the schools."

"That's good," I say. "Well, have to get going. Nice talking to you."

"Have a good trip."

Along Highway 3 south of Dunseith, I plodded along, with sore feet. Nobody stopped. One or two drivers tooted their horns. It's as if everyone was flying by at warp speed, too busy and too fast to really feel for the victims of the hurricanes.

I camped for the night on the east side of the road along a shelter belt of trees and shrubs, well protected from the west wind and the noise of the highway. I can't be seen, anyway. Tired. Just plain beat. Sore feet, three blisters. So nice to sit back and read the Minot Daily News and weekly newspaper from the little town of Rolla. I slept soundly.

Chapter 28

Ernie at the Sky Dancer

AT 11 P.M. FRIDAY I awoke, the stars bright in the heavens, visible through the thin netting of my tent. It was cool and pleasant. I slept again until – raindrops fell. I scurried out at 2:30 and put the fly over the tent. It turned out to be just a sprinkle.

By 7:15 I awoke as usual and turned on the radio. Day 6. Good weather predicted until Sunday night, when rain is expected. Think I'll go to Rolette instead of Rugby. It's more on my way and shorter. And the highway is producing no donations. I'll save 44 miles of walking and get myself home by next Saturday night, when the hockey season begins. Don't want to miss that!

It turned out to be a very good thing I cut the trip short.

On Oct. 1 another beautiful morning dawned, with hazy clouds lingering from the light rain a few hours earlier. I allowed myself a little extra time this morning -- it was a Saturday, after all -- and was gone by 8:30. The walking was easy. My right foot felt better, as the blisters had broken and hardened. I'd put some Chinese noodles into a pot with cold water the previous night and eaten half of them then, saving the rest for this morning. Tasted good.

A stiff east wind blew (a sign of changing weather on the Prairie), cars passed by, but again no stoppers. I felt a stronger conviction to head east to Rolette rather than Rugby. I stopped at 9 or so and made a fire and cooked a bannock near a line of trees. Good breakfast, with peanut butter and honey and oatmeal too.

Walking and more walking, thinking and more thinking. Don Dietrich's story would make a book. He's a Deloraine guy who lived his dream and played 10 years of professional hockey, partly with the Chicago Black Hawks, partly in the American Hockey League, and a few years in Europe. In retirement he found himself with both cancer and Parkinson's disease. Quite a shock. Quite a story, too, one that could give people hope, because he was dealing well with both illnesses.

I mulled it over and decided to make it a priority project. (Two years later the book, *No Guarantees*, was published and well received.)

I saw odd things on the roadside -- diapers, a condom, a penny, lots of Bud Light cans and fast food wrappers. Dead snakes and mice and even a bird or two ground into the pavement. A few people toot, but none stop.

Maybe tonight, if you get to Rolette, I tell myself, you can see a movie, or have a nice supper, or both. And church is tomorrow. Maybe there you can get some donations. So get your butt to Rolette and hope it's a decent little town.

I arrived about 4:30 and set up camp behind a large lot full of school buses in various stages of disrepair. My tenting site was grassy and out of sight. On Main Street there wasn't much, just a small plaza (which closed at 5) and a cafe, which I went to immediately for a bite to eat -- and was I glad I went there. The spaghetti was fantastic, and a salad bar went with it, all for $6.96. I had a chocolate shake as well. The spaghetti was so good that I asked the pretty young waitress to tell the cook that it's better than the spaghetti I had in Italy. Then a bread stick arrived, I guess his way of saying thanks.

After cleaning up a bit in the washroom, I headed over to a service station to check out bread prices (more than $2) and decided to cook up a couple of bannocks instead. Back at camp, I had a great night's sleep. I decided to pass on the movie. It started at 8, and with all this walking I couldn't stay awake much later than that.

* * *

Day 7, Sunday Oct. 2, was a super day. I finished off the spaghetti for breakfast and headed out, packed up and ready to try to some distance toward Belcourt. But first, church. A clerk in the service station told me about a Lutheran Church down State Street, which also led north to Belcourt, so there I went, hoping to maybe receive a few donations. The pastor told me they'd been giving freely to the relief effort, and were even preparing to receive a family or two. So they'd done their part.

At the church I ran into a couple of old friends from our choir days, Bob Gilje and Gary Linson. Gee it was good to see them. They sang with the Bottineau and Area Men's Choir when Gordy Lindquist ran the show, but Gordy retired from teaching and stepped down from the choir a couple of years ago, the same time Jim Smart packed it in with us, the Southwest Singers. So we don't sing together anymore, and that's too bad. It was truly an international men's chorus for a few years. We'd take turns doing concerts in each other's towns -- a lot of fun. I remember Dad attending one of them with me. He thought it was great.

"Good to see you, Brad," said Gary, a tenor and retired farmer. "Did you finish that schooling in Winnipeg?" He remembered that, of all things, my MA. What a guy.

"Yes," I told him and we had a nice chat.

"You'd best be going before the weather turns ugly," he said, and I agreed and headed out. Some rain or snow was on the way, he said.

I had misgivings. It was 12:30 and maybe I should have returned to the diner and had lunch. I was rather hoping Gary or Bob would have invited me to lunch. But I stopped among some trees and made a fire and cooked a bannock and had some beans and tuna with cold tea and it was good. A person can get too soft in these restaurants, anyway.

Man, did it cool off quickly. Coming out of the church, we figured the temperature had fallen 10 degrees F from when we had gone in. I bundled up and got the blood circulating and walked my feet off, as I wanted to do the 11 miles down to No. 5 which heads east to Belcourt.

It was depressing. Nobody stopped. I found a house close to the road -- a rare thing here believe it or not (any house is rare on this road) -- and stopped to try for some water. Jerry Laverdure was helpful and had some good water. Gave me an apple too. I took a photo of him and his dog, Duke. Duke and I got along well. Jerry works for the county on a grader and other big machines. Has for 30 years, he told me. He tried to give me a soft drink, but said his granddaughter must have drunk them all.

An hour or so later a van flew by me headed north, then turned around. It appeared to be someone from the reservation who handed me $10. I thanked him a lot. "You know, you're the first people in two days to stop and help. Thanks so much."

A couple of others stopped in the next 30 minutes, but neither made a donation. By 5 I hit the highway and half an hour later was at the casino, Sky Dancer Hotel and Casino near Belcourt. Security let me set up my tent on their grounds, and in I went for the washroom, where I bathed my sore feet. My right foot had three blisters, one on the bottom and two on toes. It felt better for being clean. As I washed, a fellow in his 50s came over and said. "Foot rot? I've had it."

I said no, just blisters.

"I had foot rot in the Nam," he continued. "It's bad. Stays on forever."

"How long were you there?"

"Eighteen months."

"It's a wonder you didn't get more than foot rot. Were you ever wounded?"

"I'm a good ducker," he said, and then switched topics.

It was outside the WC, after that, that I met a good friend coming in.

Chapter 29

Snow Threatens

"ERNIE, GREAT TO see you!"

"Bird," he said, half laughing, with a big smile. He was a neighbour and a trapping partner. I used to skin a lot of Ernie's muskrats and beavers. He paid about a buck a rat and more for a beaver. We'd spent many hours working in his fur shack, until it burned down. A bad stove pipe was to blame. We both lost stuff in the fire, but I arrived soon enough to save a number of beaver pelts I'd boarded for him, and other things.

Ernie was one of the best trappers on Turtle Mountain and I picked his brain for whatever he was willing to share, which wasn't a lot. He liked to have me figure things out for myself. Over six or seven seasons of trapping beaver, muskrats, mink, raccoons, red squirrels and coyote, we talked a lot.

"I walked here, Ernie," I told him.

"I know. It's in the Recorder."

We went into the WC and he washed his hands, and cracked a joke with a maintenance guy he obviously knew (Ernie was a good customer in that gambling establishment), and then he said, "Come on. Margaret's here too." She was busy feeding quarters into one of the machines. But she'd done OK that day.

"Have you eaten?" she asked.

I hadn't.

"Here," and she hands me a $20.

"Thanks a lot, Margaret! You're a great old gal."

"I like the 'great' part but not the 'old' part," she said.

"Sorry. You're a great gal!"

I saved the money. Using Ernie's gambling card, I picked up two hot dogs and a Pepsi for free. Gamblers eat that stuff free.

After a bit more visiting I headed out to my tent and had a good night's sleep.

* * *

On Day 8, Monday, Oct. 3, the temperature hovered around 34 degrees F or one or two Celsius when I awoke about 7. Clearly the weather had turned for the worse and I needed to be making tracks for home. But first I had business to attend to -- asking casino manager Ray Trottier to donate to the cause. The place had to be making a lot of bucks.

This, however, was easier said than done. First I went for breakfast, and had a good one. Trottier didn't come in until 9 or later, so I had some waiting to do. After eating I packed up my gear and met his secretary, a helpful woman named Anna Giron, who had recently moved there from Minot.

"He's a nice man and I'm sure he'll help."

About 9:30 he still wasn't in, and she phoned him. "Sorry, but he has to have approval for any donations from the Tribal Council," she explained. "It's just up the road and I'll tell you who to talk to."

This wasn't the best scenario for me, but I went down to the tribal office and met a man who worked for chairman Ken Davis. "Sorry, but it's year end and our budget is overspent."

"Look, I'd like to talk to the treasurer. This is important and I'm not giving up."

He led me down to Janice Azure's office. She was a council person as well as treasurer, according to the note Anna had given me. After waiting some more, I finally found her in another office, talking to two other councilors, and I made my pitch.

"At church yesterday they gave to Hurricane relief," one of the men said.

"Yes, but it all helps. I'm sure the casino could provide some help," I replied. "The Red Cross boss in Minot tells me they need more funding."

I ended up writing a letter to the council requesting a donation to the Red Cross. Janice photocopied my letter from Allan and put them together. My request and others would be considered Wednesday. It was all I could do. I never did get a donation.

Leaving the tribal council office, I headed east on Highway 5 toward Belcourt and Rolla. But I was having second thoughts about going the additional six miles or so to Rolla. What would be gained? Likely not much. And time was a factor. I don't want to get stuck in that snowstorm they were predicting for tomorrow night. That would mean a motel room and additional expenses, or possibly a very uncomfortable night in the tent.

As I strode east I decided to head north to St. John from Belcourt. If I made it to a few miles west of St. John by day's end I'd be well positioned to get home Tuesday night. This became my goal.

In the meantime the day went well. At a small supermarket approaching Belcourt a meat cutter told me: "Turn left at the second set of lights. That'll take you to St. John." On the way I stopped at a school bus garage and ate lunch inside with half a dozen men. But there was no inclination among them to support the cause.

"I don't like the Red Cross," one said. "Back in '91 I was shot, and got no help from them. Couldn't even get a month's rent out of them."

OK. I asked no further questions. He seemed to speak for them all. Lunch for me was some bannock, beans, water and almonds.

On the road again I pushed along at a good pace, up the mountainside. There was no shoulder to speak of and it was tricky on the busy road. Why so many cars? I couldn't figure it out. Somebody had quipped that St. John was so small you might blink and miss it, so they couldn't be coming from there. Then I came upon it -- a college. A large college on the west side, with a stream of vehicles in and out. Very handy if you live in Belcourt.

Also along the way I came across a native wellness centre. No building was in sight just a sign, near a pretty lake.

Then, suddenly, one of the best things of the journey took place. Two fellows in a pickup truck who had been heading north stopped, turned around and gave me $31 when I told them my cause. The biggest donation of the trip. It's the ordinary working people who are the most generous, I find. That made my day.

I did have one regret about not going to Rolla. That's the home of a very good newspaper, the *Turtle Mountain Star*, and I'd hoped to talk to them about the trip. But maybe there was yet a way to talk to them without being there. Why not phone? Stop at a home along the way here and call them. So I did.

I watched a car pull into a modest bungalow ahead on my left, and decided to try there. "Excuse me. Anybody home?"

Fifteen-year-old Jesse Stewart came out of the house. "May I please use your phone to make a local call? I'm walking to raise money for Red Cross Hurricane relief."

"Sure," and he goes for the cordless phone. He returns with his sister Kari, 4. Two dogs also greeted me, Charley and Blue. Charley is in the photo I took of them. I got through to the *Star* and was told a reporter would be out to meet me on the road. I also called the *Times* of Belcourt and left a message for a reporter there.

Jesse and I chatted for a few minutes as I told him about the trip. A pleasant young man. On the entire trip I had no ill-will from anyone, really. Some just couldn't help out, but that was understandable.

I felt much better having phoned the *Star*, and set off with renewed energy. Hardly 10 minutes had passed before a little red car pulled up ahead. John Rosinski was the reporter, a man in his early 20s. He took a few photos and then I asked him if he wanted me inside the car for the interview. No, he said, he'd come out with me. But it was cold.

The interview went well. "I'm cold," he said. He took a photo with my camera, and then he headed off. He said he'd phone me Thursday at home.

Yes, I felt much better after that. Now it was just a matter of getting to St. John, and by about 4 p.m. I did. One of the first impressions of the pretty little village was a line of purple hollyhocks near the sidewalk. Mom had hollyhocks at home in Toronto. She'd passed away in January 1997 at age 76. My Border to the Bay walk had been inspired by her, as she'd suffered from heart disease and stroke.

I stopped to photograph and admire the plants, and the lady of the house appeared. Margaret was chatty and friendly and we had a good visit. I told her about the hollyhocks I'd grown up with as a kid, and she showed me another miniature variety that I didn't even know existed.

Although I wasn't really hungry, I thought it would be a good idea to have a restaurant meal if one could be had, so that I could keep walking with energy.

"There's a cafe attached to the bar down the road," she said, and boy it was a good one. A man named Richard was behind the counter and he served up a lovely bowl of homemade barley soup and a cheese omelet. I got the works, plus a couple of carrot cake muffins (which I kept in reserve), for $2.50. Now my tank was full.

But the day wasn't done yet. I still had some miles to go before I slept. For all I knew I'd be walking in snow the next day, Tuesday, though I sure hoped not. I wanted to be as far along as I could.

Chapter 30

Home

AT THE INTERSECTION where I turned west I saw a man riding a tractor and pulling a grass cutter for the shoulders, so I snapped a photo of him.

The landscape along this road was beautiful -- undulating hills, glorious colours, a painter's paradise. But I had no time to paint (though my watercolours were with me). I pushed on, admiring the golden hues and gentle slopes and curious cattle and by 6 p.m. came upon a farm and a farmer pulling out of his drive. It was the grass cutter.

"Good to see you again," this friendly fellow said, and he gave me his name – Oscar Haas.

"I work for the county, have for 22 years. What's up?"

I explained my trip.

"You're welcome to camp on my land if you like."

"Thanks," I said, "it's about time to quit. Maybe just over there," and I pointed.

He talked about the good quality water in the nearby well, and how he'd gone through a carpentry course upon graduation from high school. Then he'd become ill. Diagnosis? Allergic to sawdust.

"So I got this county job and it's been good. But they'll be mad at me for not getting all the grass cut if it snows."

"Surely they won't hold it against you."

"Oh, they will. There's a lot of grass to cut. I work a 4-10 shift, four days on, four off. My last four off my son and I were cutting and hauling hay, nonstop. You know there's room in the house if you wanted to sleep inside."

"Thanks, but I'm comfortable outside."

"OK. After I check these cattle the boy and I are cutting firewood. Still haven't got our wood in."

"I burn wood too, and am in the same boat. Anyway, good meeting you, Oscar." And we parted.

Through the barbed-wire gate I found 20 or so round bales and positioned my tent to afford the greatest protection from north and west winds. I was close to the road but couldn't be seen, out of the wind and safe. Sweet. Soon I was asleep.

* * *

On Day 9, Tuesday Oct. 4, by a strange coincidence I hit the highway at 10 to 8 a.m., the same moment Oscar Haas drove his pickup out of the yard toward his county job three miles away in St. John.

Today, God willing, I would enter Canada by mid-afternoon and be home by supper time. But I had to hoof it to make this happen. There was no snow yet, or rain. I'd heard some sprinkles on the tent in the night but it didn't amount to anything. It was plus one C or 34 F when I got up.

From St. John to the Peace Garden customs office was 20 miles, so I figured I had 16 or 17 miles to go, and at three miles per hour that meant an arrival time of about 1:30. By this time I was eager to get back on Canadian turf. I hadn't bought any medical insurance. I'd had no trouble, but didn't believe in pushing my luck.

I plodded on, and kept up a robotic pace that I'd learned during my trek to Churchill. (That was 1,620 kilometres, about 1,000 miles, Jan. 25 to April 15 or so of 2005.) It's as if your legs aren't really part of you. They don't feel, they don't hurt, they just walk and walk and walk and run down the hills and walk up the slopes and keep going regardless, because they have to. The three blisters on my right foot were not an issue. Walk walk walk.

I'd eaten some bannock and one of the carrot cakes before even getting out of the sack. Every little while I'd eat a bit more. On walks, I didn't eat three square meals; I'd eat a little every couple of hours.

At one point I came across a pretty farm with a man and two dogs to my left and shouted a hello. He told me I had seven miles to go until the intersection of No. 3 Highway.

"No problem," I shouted, and I'm not sure he believed me. Most people walk very little, and seven miles is a considerable distance.

I got to the stop sign a bit after 12. It felt good. Northward I turned, up the longest and steepest hill of the trip. Part way up south-bound pickup truck stops in front of me. It's Keith Burton, my former colleague at the Peace Garden, the maintenance boss. He had a big smile on his face as usual.

"How's it going?" he asked.

"Well, I'm almost done. Thank goodness. Storm's coming." It was good to see him.

Not five minutes later another truck came toward me and I waved (I waved at most of the drivers I saw). This one drove past, then stopped and swung around. Border Patrol, a federal officer. On this trip I'd seen a sheriff, two border patrol men, two customs officers, and one sheriff who didn't bother to stop.

"Your papers, please." I handed over my passport. He phoned in to have me checked out and I came up clean.

"Would you care to make a donation?" I thought this was a tad brassy on my part. He responded by saying he didn't think it would be appropriate since he was on duty.

"Sheriff Watson of Bottineau gave me $10 for the cause." Bird, you don't give up real easy, do you.

"He's local. I'm federal." I don't know what difference that makes and didn't ask. "This is quite a hill," he said.

I agreed. "Thanks for stopping and chatting. And keep up the good work," I said. And he was gone.

One less obstacle to overcome before I am home. One less thing that can go wrong.

At the hilltop I encountered the fieldstone fence posts that mark out the Peace Garden's territory and knew I was very close now. Plod on, and it's only about 1:30. I strode past the U.S. Customs office toward the Canadian gate feeling good, feeling like I'd got somewhere. The two men at the port knew me, and I knew them by face if not by name, and one filled me in on a murder than had been committed in Boissevain two days earlier. I didn't know either the deceased or the accused, but such an event is rare.

Inside, I pulled out my passport. "There's a paper here they want you to return," I said, showing them. It was my date of departure sheet. "They said I could turn it in myself but I've seen plenty enough dark blue uniforms in the past seven days to last me a lifetime. Mind you they were all respectful and professional," I stressed.

"Really? Not everyone says that."

"They were to me." I cleaned up a bit and phoned Rheinhardt Wiebe, a friend just up the road. He was babysitting the triplets and his older boy while Leanne was in town but said he'd give me a lift across the park to Canada Corner. That's 12 miles. Otherwise I'd never make it home that night. For me, the fundraiser ended the minute I entered Canada. It was an American thing for Americans. Now I was home.

I was a pretty happy camper as I hoofed it past customs toward my familiar Turtle Mountain Provincial Park, where I'd worked the previous four summers. It was still cold and overcast but not raining or snowing and it appeared the storm would hold off until later that night. Thank goodness. I needed to haul in some firewood, find the cats and put away my gear, then have a hot bath.

Man, I craved a hot bath, not having showered or bathed for nine days. What I did do was wash my hair twice and sponge bath in restaurant washrooms, but it's not the same. I craved a hot bath and was so close I could feel it.

Rheinhardt pulled up about 45 minutes later, as I approached the entrance to Adam Lake, and he was in his van. I didn't like the look of that. I thought he'd drive the big Suburban. We got the Action Packers and whatnot inside the van OK and hoisted the buggy on the roof rack, strapping it down with bungee cords. Big mistake. A mile down the road the cords broke and the buggy hit the highway flying. Or should I say bouncing. It bent a bit. One wheel and the copper pipe basket bent a little, and Al Thio came along in a Parks truck and we loaded it up and he drove it to Rheinhardt's place a tad further, where we bent it back as best we could so that it rolled well. I felt bad about that, and should have made sure it was tied down properly with rope. Sorry, Dave. (My neighbour Dave Wall, a real genius, had made it from stuff from the dump.)

"Leanne said to invite you in for a cup of hot chocolate but you likely want to head right home."

"I do. Thank her for me and tell her I'll take a rain check, but I need to get cleaned up and I'll still have four miles to cover when you drop me at Canada Corner."

He showed me fantastic video footage of a bull elk he called the other day. It came to within 20 feet of him, he said, and it called its bugle-like call. All on video. We talked of trapping and hunting and whatnot as we drove along the West Main Trail in the park, a winding wilderness pathway originally cut as a firebreak in the 1930s. Dad had been a part of that. He'd have been in his teens at the time. He also helped with some of the spruce plantations.

At Canada Corner we unloaded the buggy. "I want to see that thing roll," Rheinhardt said. It rolled great, and I was off, after thanking him for the help. "If you hadn't carried me here I'd have had to camp at Lake Max and likely would freeze my you-know-whats off tonight." He smiled and left. As it turned out, what I'd said was true, as the Colorado low moved in around midnight with plunging temperatures and heavy snow.

I'd stopped at Bill and Esther's for tea on my way out from home last Monday, and they'd asked me to stop back in on the way back. During my Churchill walk I also stopped in for tea and cake and we all enjoyed the visits. They were home and invited me to stay for a bite of her home-made rhubarb cake and tea, and since it was just after 4 I had time and we had a good visit. I shared some of the events of the trip and expressed my pleasure to be home again.

By six I really was home again. Pulling into the street where the Walls and I live, I stopped for a quick chat with Dave and Madeleine to let them know I was back. Like the Canadas, they seemed pleased. I know I was! And who should greet me soon after I opened the door of my mobile home? Kali. She came out of the bush. Jimmy followed an hour or two later. Where was Buddy? Not in the fur shack. But she was a hunter and wanderer and I figured she was fine. The next morning, in the height of the snowstorm, I found her curled up on my bed in the shack, picked her up and brought her inside where the fireplace was hot and welcoming. With all three cats safe and sound beside me I truly was home. And it doesn't get any better than that.

* * *

All told, with all that walking, I picked up $98 for the cause in North Dakota. I added $2 to even it up. This I then sent to the Red Cross, with this letter:

October 5, 2005

P. O. Box 871
Deloraine, MB
R0M 0M0
Canada

American Red Cross
Mid-Dakota Chapter
2021 4th Ave. NW
P.O. Box 456
Minot, ND 58702

Dear Mr. McGeough,

I arrived home yesterday from my walk through North Dakota to raise money for the Red Cross Hurricane relief effort. It took me nine days and I went about 150 miles. Fortunately I got home before the snowstorm struck. I started from my home in Canada on the north shore of Lake Metigoshe on Sept. 26. My journey took me through the Carbury Port (to which you faxed a letter on my behalf) to Bottineau, Dunseith, south to Rolette, north to Belcourt, St. John, and home through the Peace Garden port.

Along the way I tented and was interviewed by Dylan Connor of Sunny 101.9 or KBTO radio, Scott Wagar of the Bottineau Courant and John Rosinski of the Turtle Mountain Star. In each case I encouraged people to donate to the Red Cross relief effort ("Bird's walk for Hurricane relief") and provided the toll-free phone number. I also made a pitch to the Turtle Mountain Chippewa Tribal Council for them to donate. On Oct. 3 I met with tribal council treasurer Janice Azure and a couple of councilors and left a letter requesting a donation for you.

Allan, there was a third way I raised funds for you -- cash donations. As I walked along, pulling my buggy with my gear with a sign "Support Hurricane Relief," people occasionally stopped and donated. I kept track of each one. There were 13 donations totaling $98. I'll add $2 to bring it to $100. The first to donate was Sheriff Steve Watson of Bottineau ($10). The largest donation was $31 by two men in a pickup truck north of Belcourt. The smallest was $1. Attached is a list.

The people of North Dakota were friendly and respectful toward this Manitoban. Restaurants typically gave me meals for half price. In Rolette, I met two gentlemen I used to sing with in an international choir led by Gordy Lindquist. I enjoyed the walk very much. Keep up the good work!

Sincerely,

Brad Bird.